CentOS High Performance

Create high availability clusters to enhance system performance using CentOS 7

Gabriel Cánepa

BIRMINGHAM - MUMBAI

CentOS High Performance

Copyright © 2016 Packt Publishing

All rights reserved. No part of this book may be reproduced, stored in a retrieval system, or transmitted in any form or by any means, without the prior written permission of the publisher, except in the case of brief quotations embedded in critical articles or reviews.

Every effort has been made in the preparation of this book to ensure the accuracy of the information presented. However, the information contained in this book is sold without warranty, either express or implied. Neither the author nor Packt Publishing, and its dealers and distributors will be held liable for any damages caused or alleged to be caused directly or indirectly by this book.

Packt Publishing has endeavored to provide trademark information about all of the companies and products mentioned in this book by the appropriate use of capitals. However, Packt Publishing cannot guarantee the accuracy of this information.

First published: January 2016

Production reference: 1250116

Published by Packt Publishing Ltd.
Livery Place
35 Livery Street
Birmingham B3 2PB, UK.

ISBN 978-1-78528-868-5

www.packtpub.com

Credits

Author
Gabriel Cánepa

Reviewers
Muhammad Kamran Azeem
Denis Fateyev
Lekshminarayanan K
Oliver Pelz

Commissioning Editor
Veena Pagare

Acquisition Editor
Subho Gupta

Content Development Editor
Zeeyan Pinheiro

Technical Editor
Vivek Pala

Copy Editor
Pranjali Chury

Project Coordinator
Suzanne Coutinho

Proofreader
Safis Editing

Indexer
Mariammal Chettiyar

Graphics
Disha Haria

Production Coordinator
Nilesh Mohite

Cover Work
Nilesh Mohite

About the Author

Gabriel Cánepa is a Linux Foundation certified system administrator (LFCS-1500-0576-0100) and web developer from Villa Mercedes, San Luis, Argentina. He works for a worldwide leading consumer product company and takes great pleasure in using FOSS tools to increase productivity in all areas of his daily work. When he's not typing commands or writing code or articles, he enjoys telling bedtime stories with his wife to his two little daughters and playing with them, which is a great pleasure in his life.

> I would like to thank God for the many blessings and the growth opportunities in personal, family, and professional life that He has given throughout my life.
>
> I would like to thank my mother, who always encouraged me to get as much education as possible and to excel in everything I do. I'd also like to thank my wife, Monica, and our two daughters, Camila and Francesca, for their support, understanding, and patience during the long hours of troubleshooting and writing this book.
>
> Next, I'd like to thank Andrea de Ampalio and Diego Cordoba from Carrera Linux Argentina (`www.carreralinux.com.ar`), who helped me learn and love Linux in the best Linux training academy—their people and Linux skills are without match, and Subho Gupta, Manasi Pandire, Zeeyan Pinheiro and Vivek Pala from Packt Publishing for their remarkable talent and support while we worked together on this book.
>
> Last but not least, I'd like to thank Andrew Beekhoff and the team at Cluster Labs (`http://clusterlabs.org/`) for putting together the best and most complete cluster resource information guide out there, which served as the main source of my research.

About the Reviewers

Muhammad Kamran Azeem is a seasoned IT professional with twenty years of experience in IT. He started working as a PC technician in 1995 and gradually got into database administration, system administration, high performance computing, and, lately, information security. He also taught undergraduate and graduate level courses for C/C++, data structures and algorithm design, Oracle developer, and a lot more, in different universities in Pakistan.

Kamran holds a master's degree in IT, and is certified under CISSP, CEH, RHCE, OCP, and CCNA programs. He is the author of Pakistan's first book on Linux system administration titled *Linux Pocket Reference for System*.

Administrators, and many training videos on using Linux as the main desktop operating system, as well as Linux system administration, all available through his website `http://wbitt.com`.

He is an advocate of Free and Open Source Software (FOSS), and for the last ten years, he is the driving force behind the wave of adaptation of Linux in Pakistan.

He is currently working as a senior DevOps consultant for Praqma AS in Oslo, Norway, helping companies adopt modern software and IT infrastructure practices.

> First, I would like to thank my wife, Rohina, for being the greatest support in what I do. I would also like to thank Mike Long, my employer, for encouraging me to undertake this book review project.

Denis Fateyev holds a master's degree in Computer Science and has been working with Linux for more than 10 years (mostly with RedHat and CentOS). He currently works as a Perl programmer and DevOps for a small German company. He has reviewed several books mostly related to CentOS, DevOps, and high availability technologies, including *GitLab Cookbook*, *CentOS High Availability*, *CentOS High Performance* by Packt Publishing. Being a keen participant in the open source community, he is a package maintainer at Fedora and Repoforge projects. He has a passion for foreign languages, namely, German and Spanish, and linguistics.

He can be reached at `denis@fateyev.com`.

Lekshminarayanan K has been administering Linux/Unix servers since 2009. He had his first experience with the open source on Ubuntu 8.04 ever since then he has experienced many flavors of Linux like CentOS, Red-hat, Fedora and Debian. Lekshminarayan is also experienced in application administrations like Apache, Qmail, SVN, and GIT. He is currently teaching himself Shell and Python scripting and working as a Linux administrator at COMODO Inc.

During his free time, he enjoys photography and is too fond of books.

Oliver Pelz has more than 10 years of experience as a software developer and system administrator. He graduated with a diploma in Bioinformatics and is currently working at the German Cancer Research center in Heidelberg, where he has authored and coauthored several scientific publications in the field of Bioinformatics. Next to developing web applications and biological databases for his department and scientists all over the world, he is administrating a division-wide Linux-based data center and has set up two high-performance CentOS clusters for the analysis of high-throughput microscope and genome sequencing data. He loves writing code, riding his mountain bike in the Black Forest of Germany and is an absolute Linux and open source enthusiast for many years. He has contributed to several open source projects in the past and is also the author of the book *CentOS 7 Linux Server Cookbook*, Packt Publishing. He maintains an IT tech blog at www.oliverpelz.de.

> I would like to thank my family and especially my wonderful wife Beatrice and little son Jonah for their patience and understanding for all these long working hours and the folks at Packt Publishing for the opportunity to review this manuscript, it was a great pleasure for me.

www.PacktPub.com

Support files, eBooks, discount offers, and more

For support files and downloads related to your book, please visit `www.PacktPub.com`.

Did you know that Packt offers eBook versions of every book published, with PDF and ePub files available? You can upgrade to the eBook version at `www.PacktPub.com` and as a print book customer, you are entitled to a discount on the eBook copy. Get in touch with us at `service@packtpub.com` for more details.

At `www.PacktPub.com`, you can also read a collection of free technical articles, sign up for a range of free newsletters and receive exclusive discounts and offers on Packt books and eBooks.

`https://www2.packtpub.com/books/subscription/packtlib`

Do you need instant solutions to your IT questions? PacktLib is Packt's online digital book library. Here, you can search, access, and read Packt's entire library of books.

Why subscribe?

- Fully searchable across every book published by Packt
- Copy and paste, print, and bookmark content
- On demand and accessible via a web browser

Free access for Packt account holders

If you have an account with Packt at `www.PacktPub.com`, you can use this to access PacktLib today and view 9 entirely free books. Simply use your login credentials for immediate access.

Table of Contents

Preface	**v**
Chapter 1: Cluster Basics and Installation on CentOS 7	**1**
Clustering fundamentals	**1**
Why Linux and CentOS 7?	2
Downloading CentOS	3
Setting up CentOS 7 nodes	**4**
Installing CentOS 7	5
Setting up the network infrastructure	7
Installing the packages required for clustering	**10**
Key software components	11
Setting up key-based authentication for SSH access	14
Summary	**16**
Chapter 2: Installing Cluster Services and Configuring Network Components	**17**
Configuring and starting clustering services	**18**
Starting and enabling clustering services	18
Troubleshooting	20
Security fundamentals	**20**
Letting in and letting out	21
Getting acquainted with PCS	**25**
Managing authentication and creating the cluster	28
Setting up a virtual IP for the cluster	**33**
Adding a virtual IP as a cluster resource	33
Viewing the status of the virtual IP	34
Summary	**35**

Table of Contents

Chapter 3: A Closer Look at High Availability — 37
- Failover – an introduction to high availability and performance — 38
- Fencing – isolating the malfunctioning nodes — 43
- Installing and configuring a STONITH device — 45
- Split-brain – preparing to avoid inconsistencies — 49
- Quorum – scoring inside your cluster — 49
- Configuring our cluster with PCS GUI — 51
- Summary — 53

Chapter 4: Real-world Implementations of Clustering — 55
- Setting up storage — 55
- ELRepo repository and DRBD availability — 58
- Configuring DRBD — 60
- Adding DRBD as a PCS cluster resource — 66
- Installing the web and database servers — 70
- Configuring the web server as a cluster resource — 72
- Mounting the DRBD resource and using it with Apache — 76
- Testing the DRBD resource along with Apache — 79
- Setting up a high-availability database with replicated storage — 80
- Troubleshooting — 85
- Summary — 87

Chapter 5: Monitoring the Cluster Health — 89
- Cluster services and performance — 89
- Monitoring the node status — 89
- Monitoring the resources — 92
  - When a resource refuses to start — 98
  - Checking the availability of core components — 100
- Summary — 102

Chapter 6: Measuring and Increasing Performance — 103
- Setting up a sample database — 103
  - Downloading and installing the Employees database — 104
- Introducing initial cluster tests — 108
  - Test 1 – retrieving all fields from all records — 109
  - Test 2 – performing JOIN operations — 110
  - Performing a failover — 111
- Measuring and improving performance — 113
  - Apache's configuration and settings — 113
  - Loading and disabling modules — 115
  - Placing limits on the number of Apache processes and children — 115

Database resource	116
Creating indexes	116
Using query cache	117
Moving to an A/A cluster	**119**
Summary	**122**
Index	**123**

Preface

CentOS is the enterprise level Linux OS, which is 100% binary compatible with Red Hat Enterprise Linux (RHEL). It acts as a free alternative to RedHat's commercial Linux offering, with only a change in the branding. A high performance cluster consists of a group of computers that work together as one set parallel, hence minimizing or eliminating the downtime of critical services and enhancing the performance of the application.

What this book covers

Chapter 1, Cluster Basics and Installation on CentOS 7, reviews the basic principles of clustering and outlines the necessary steps to install a cluster with two CentOS 7 servers.

Chapter 2, Installing Cluster Services and Configuring Network Components, coversetting up and configuring the basic required network infrastructure and clustering services.

Chapter 3, A Closer Look at High Availability, lists the components of a cluster in detail and demonstrates how to approach the split-brain problem by configuring the failover and fencing the cluster as a whole and the quorum of each node individually.

Chapter 4, Real-world Implementations of Clustering, covers how to implement a web server and a database server in your cluster.

Chapter 5, Monitoring the Cluster Health, talks about how to monitor the performance and availability of your cluster.

Chapter 6, Measuring and Increasing Performance, reviews performance tuning techniques for your recently installed high availability cluster.

What you need for this book

To follow along with this book, you will need to download a CentOS 7 minimal install image from the project's website. You will be asked to install other packages (pacemaker, corosync, and pcs, to name a few examples) in each chapter as required.

Who this book is for

This book is directed toward two groups of system administrators—those who want a detailed, step-by-step guide to setting up a high-performance and high-availability CentOS 7 cluster and those who are looking for a reference book to help them learn the necessary skills to ensure that their systems and the corresponding resources, and services are being utilized at their best capacity. No previous knowledge of performance tuning is needed to start reading this book, but the reader is expected to have at least some degree of familiarity with any spin-off of the Fedora family of Linux distributions, preferably CentOS.

Conventions

In this book, you will find a number of styles of text that distinguish between different kinds of information. Here are some examples of these styles, and an explanation of their meaning.

Code words in text, database table names, folder names, filenames, file extensions, pathnames, dummy URLs, user input, and Twitter handles are shown as follows. To download the Employees table, go to `https://launchpad.net/testdb/`:

A block of code is set as follows:

```
HWADDR="08:00:27:C8:C2:BE"
TYPE="Ethernet"
BOOTPROTO="static"
NAME="enp0s3"
ONBOOT="yes"
IPADDR="192.168.0.2"
NETMASK="255.255.255.0"
```

New terms and **important words** are shown in bold. Words that you see on the screen, in menus or dialog boxes for example, appear in the text like this: "Highlight **Install CentOS 7** using the up and down arrows ".

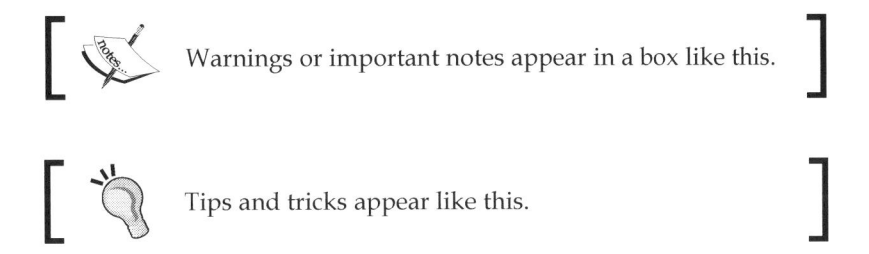

> Warnings or important notes appear in a box like this.

> Tips and tricks appear like this.

Reader feedback

Feedback from our readers is always welcome. Let us know what you think about this book—what you liked or may have disliked. Reader feedback is important for us to develop titles that you really get the most out of.

To send us general feedback, simply send an e-mail to feedback@packtpub.com, and mention the book title via the subject of your message.

If there is a topic that you have expertise in and you are interested in either writing or contributing to a book, see our author guide on www.packtpub.com/authors.

Customer support

Now that you are the proud owner of a Packt book, we have a number of things to help you to get the most from your purchase.

Downloading the example code

You can download the example code files for all Packt books you have purchased from your account at http://www.packtpub.com. If you purchased this book elsewhere, you can visit http://www.packtpub.com/support and register to have the files e-mailed directly to you.

Errata

Although we have taken every care to ensure the accuracy of our content, mistakes do happen. If you find a mistake in one of our books—maybe a mistake in the text or the code—we would be grateful if you would report this to us. By doing so, you can save other readers from frustration and help us improve subsequent versions of this book. If you find any errata, please report them by visiting http://www.packtpub.com/submit-errata, selecting your book, clicking on the **errata submission form** link, and entering the details of your errata. Once your errata are verified, your submission will be accepted and the errata will be uploaded on our website, or added to any list of existing errata, under the Errata section of that title. Any existing errata can be viewed by selecting your title from http://www.packtpub.com/support.

Piracy

Piracy of copyright material on the Internet is an ongoing problem across all media. At Packt, we take the protection of our copyright and licenses very seriously. If you come across any illegal copies of our works, in any form, on the Internet, please provide us with the location address or website name immediately so that we can pursue a remedy.

Please contact us at copyright@packtpub.com with a link to the suspected pirated material.

We appreciate your help in protecting our authors, and our ability to bring you valuable content.

Questions

You can contact us at questions@packtpub.com if you are having a problem with any aspect of the book, and we will do our best to address it.

Cluster Basics and Installation on CentOS 7

In this chapter, we will introduce the basic principles of clustering and show how to set up two Linux servers as members of a cluster, step by step.

As part of this process, we will install the CentOS 7 Linux distribution from scratch, along with the necessary packages, and finally configure key-based authentication for SSH access from one computer to the other. All commands, except if noted otherwise, must be run as root and are indicated by a leading $ sign throughout this book.

Clustering fundamentals

In computer science, a cluster consists of a group of computers (with each computer referred to as a **node** or **member**) that work together so that the set is seen as a single system from the outside.

The enterprise and science environments often require high computing power to analyze massive amounts of data produced every day, and redundancy. In order for the results to be always available to people either using those services or managing them, we rely on the high availability and performance of computer systems. The need of Internet websites, such as those used by banks and other commercial institutions, to perform well when under a significant load is a clear example of the advantages of using clusters.

There are two typical cluster setups. The first one involves assigning a different task to each node, thus achieving a higher performance compared with several tasks being performed by a single member on its own. Another classic use of clustering is to help ensure high availability by providing failover capabilities to the set where one node may automatically replace a failed member to minimize the downtime of one or several critical services. In either case, the concept of clustering implies not only taking advantage of the computing functionality of each member alone, but also maximizing it by complementing it with the others.

This type of cluster setup is called **high availability** (**HA**), and it aims to eliminate system downtime by failing over services from one node to another in case one of them experiences an issue that renders it inoperative. As opposed to switchover, which requires human intervention, a failover procedure is performed automatically by the cluster without any downtime. In other words, this operation is transparent to end users and clients from outside the cluster.

The second setup uses its nodes to perform operations in parallel in order to enhance the performance of one or more applications, and is called a **high-performance cluster** (**HPC**). HPCs are typically seen in scenarios involving applications and processes that use large collections of data.

Why Linux and CentOS 7?

As mentioned earlier, we will build a cluster with two machines running Linux. This choice is supported by the fact that this involves low costs and stability associated with this setup—no paid operating system or software licenses, along with the possibility of running Linux on systems with small resources (such as a Raspberry Pi or relatively old hardware). Thus, we can set up a cluster with very little resources or money.

We will begin our own journey toward clustering by setting up the separate nodes that will make up our system. Our choice of operating system is Linux and CentOS version 7, as the distribution, which is the latest available release of CentOS as of now. The binary compatibility with Red Hat Enterprise Linux © (which is one of the most well-used distributions in enterprise and scientific environments) along with its well-proven stability are the reasons behind this decision.

> CentOS 7 is available for download, free of charge, from the project's web site at http://www.centos.org/. In addition to this, specific details about the release can always be consulted in release notes available through the CentOS wiki, http://wiki.centos.org/Manuals/ReleaseNotes/CentOS7.

Downloading CentOS

To download CentOS, go to `http://www.centos.org/download/` and click on one of the three options outlined in the following screenshot:

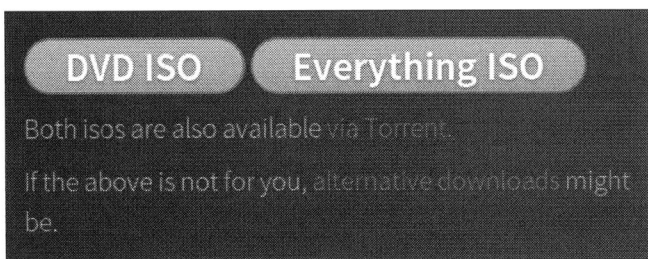

- **DVD ISO**: This is an `.iso` file (~4 GB) that can be written into regular DVD optical media and includes the common tools. Download this file if you have permanent access to a reliable Internet connection that you can use to download other packages and utilities later.
- **Everything ISO**: This is an `.iso` file (~7 GB) with the complete set of packages made available in the base repository of CentOS 7. Download this file if you do not have access to a permanent Internet connection or if your plan contemplates the possibility of installing or populating a local or network mirror.
- **alternative downloads**: This link will take you to a public directory within an official nearby CentOS mirror where the previous options are available along with others, including different choices of desktop versions (GNOME or KDE), and the minimal `.iso` file (~570 MB), which contains the core or essential packages of the distribution.

Although all the three download options will work, we will use the minimal install as it is sufficient for our purpose at hand, and we can install other needed packages using public software package repositories with the **standard Centos package manager yum** later. The recommended `.iso` file to download is the latest that is available from the download page, which at the time of writing this is **CentOS 7.0 1406 x86_64 Minimal.iso**.

Setting up CentOS 7 nodes

If you do not have dedicated hardware that you can use to set up the nodes of your cluster, you can still create them using virtual machines over some virtualization software, such as Oracle Virtualbox © or VMware ©, for example. Using virtualization will allow us to easily set up the second node after setting up the first by cloning it. The only limitation in this case is that we will not have a STONITH device available. **Shoot The Other Node In The Head (STONITH)** is a mechanism that aims to prevent two nodes from acting as the primary node in an HA cluster, thus avoiding the possibility of data corruption.

The following setup is going to be performed on a Virtualbox VM with 1 GB of RAM and 30 GB of disk space plus two network card interfaces. The first one will allow us to reach the Internet to download other packages, whereas the second will be needed to create a shared IP address to reach the cluster as a whole.

The reason why I have chosen VirtualBox over VMware is that the former is free of cost and is available for Microsoft Windows, Linux, and MacOS, while a full version of the latter costs money.

To download and install VirtualBox, go to https://www.virtualbox.org/ and choose the version for your operating system. For the installation instructions, you can refer to https://www.virtualbox.org/manual/UserManual.html, especially sections *1.7 Creating your first virtual machine*, and *1.13 Cloning virtual machines*.

Other than that, you will also need to ensure that your virtual machine has two network interface cards. The first one is created by default while the second one has to be created manually.

To display the current network configuration for a VM, click on it in Virtualbox's main interface and then on the **Settings** button. A popup window will appear with the list of the different hardware categories. Choose **Network** and configure **Adapter 1** to **Bridged Adapter**, as shown in the following screenshot:

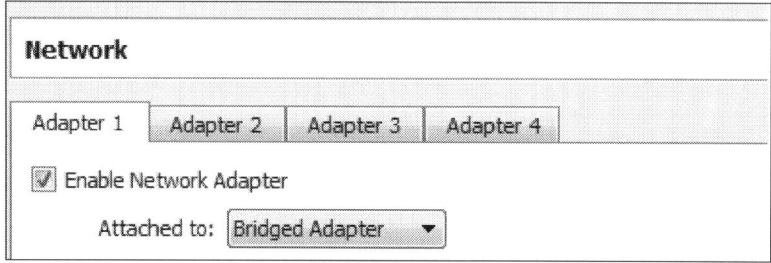

Click on **Adapter 2**, enable it by checking the corresponding checkbox and configure it as part of an **Internal Network** named **intnet**, as shown in the following screenshot:

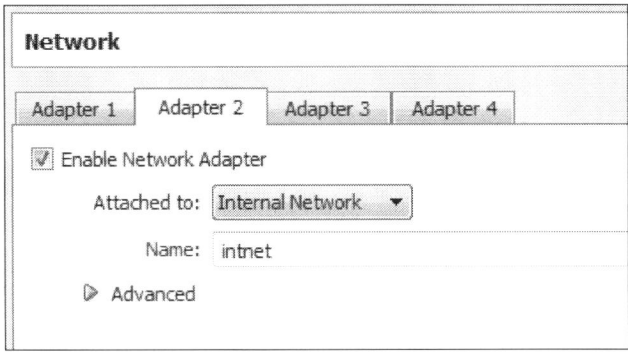

We will use the default partitioning schema (LVM) as suggested by the installation process.

Installing CentOS 7

We will start by creating the first node step by step and then use the cloning feature in Virtualbox to instantiate an identical node. This will reduce the necessary time for the installation as it will only require a slight modification to the hostname and network. Follow these steps to install CentOS 7 in a virtual machine:

1. The splash screen shown in the following screenshot is the first step in the installation process after loading the installation media on boot. Highlight **Install CentOS 7** using the up and down arrows and press *Enter*:

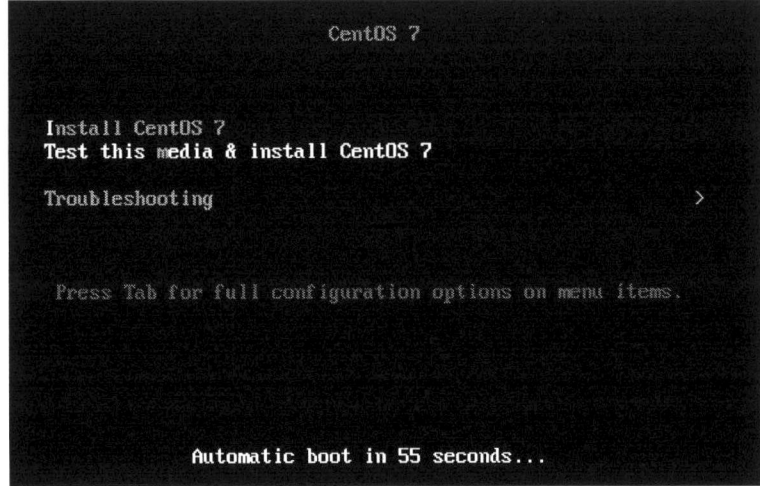

2. Select **English** (or your preferred installation language) and click on **Continue**:

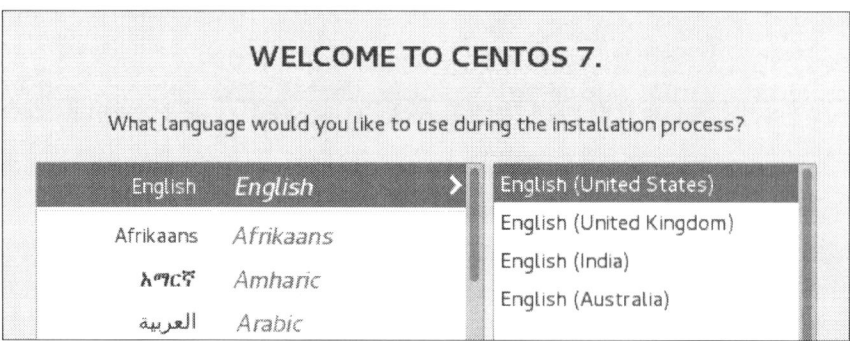

3. In the next screen, you can set the current date and time, choose a keyboard layout and language support, pick a hard drive destination for the installation along with a partitioning method, connect the main network interface, and assign a unique hostname for the node. We will name the current node as **node01** and leave the rest of the settings as default (we will configure the extra network card later). Then, click on the **Begin installation** button.

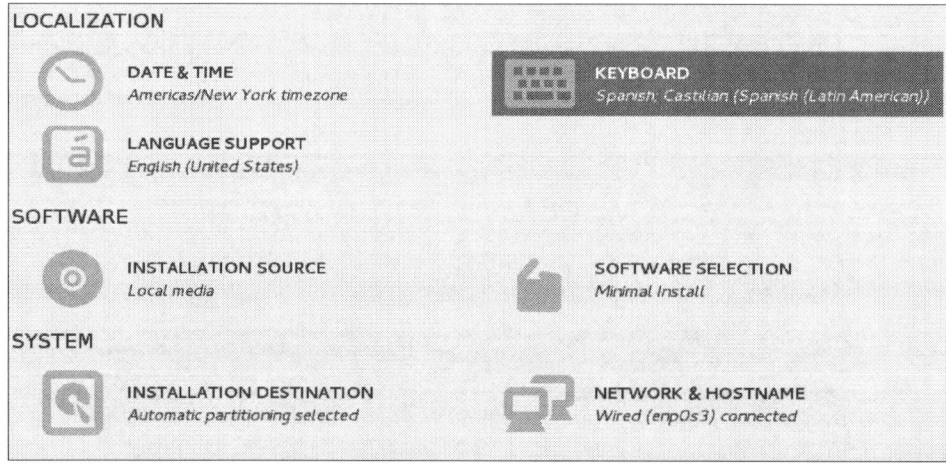

4. While the installation continues in the background, we will be prompted to set the password for the root account and create an administrative user for the node. Once these steps have been confirmed, the corresponding warnings will no longer appear:

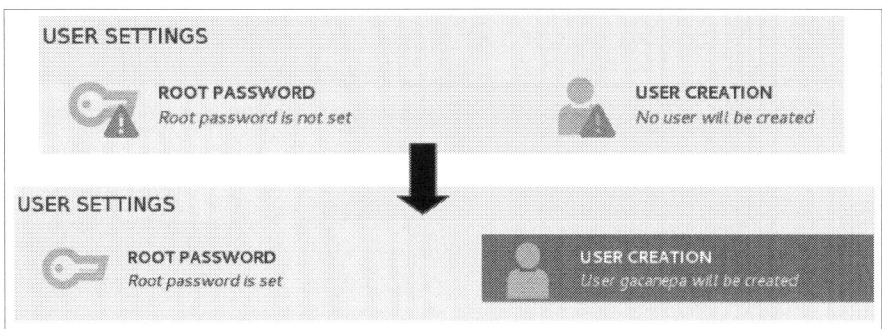

5. When the process is completed, click on **Finish configuration** and the installation will finish configuring the system and the devices. When the system is ready to boot on its own, you will be prompted to do so. Remove the installation media and click on **Reboot**.

6. After successfully restarting the computer and booting into a Linux prompt, our first task will be to update our system. However, before we can do this, we first have to set up our basic network adapter to access the Internet to download and update packages. Then, we will be able to proceed with setting up our network interfaces.

Setting up the network infrastructure

Since our nodes will communicate between each other over the network, we will first define our network addresses and configuration. Our rather basic network infrastructure will consist of two CentOS 7 boxes with static IP addresses and host names node01 [192.168.0.2] and node02 [192.168.0.3], and a gateway router called **simply gateway [192.168.0.1]**.

In CentOS, all network interfaces are configured using scripts in the /etc/sysconfig/network-scripts directory. If you followed the steps outlined earlier to create a second network interface, you should have a ifcfg-enp0s3 and ifcfg-enp0s8 file inside that directory. The first one is the configuration file for the network card that we will use to access the Internet and to connect via SSH using an outside client, whereas the second will be used in a later chapter to be a part of a cluster resource. Note that the exact naming of the network interfaces may differ a little, but it is safe to assume that they will follow the ifcfg-enp0sX format, where X is an integer number.

This is the minimum content that is needed in the `/etc/sysconfig/network-scripts/ifcfg-enp0s3` directory for our purposes in our first node (when you set up the second node later, just change the IP address (IPADDR) to `192.168.0.3`):

```
HWADDR="08:00:27:C8:C2:BE"
TYPE="Ethernet"
BOOTPROTO="static"
NAME="enp0s3"
ONBOOT="yes"
IPADDR="192.168.0.2"
NETMASK="255.255.255.0"
GATEWAY="192.168.0.1"
PEERDNS="yes"
DNS1="8.8.8.8"
DNS2="8.8.4.4"
```

Note that the `UUID` and `HWADDR` values will be different in your case as they are assigned as part of the underlying hardware. For this reason, it is safe to leave the default values for those settings. In addition to this, beware that cluster machines need to be assigned a static IP address—never leave that up to DHCP! In the configuration file used previously, we are using Google's DNS but if you wish to, feel free to use another DNS.

When you are done making changes, save the file and restart the network service in order to apply them. Since CentOS, beginning with version 7, uses systemd instead of SysVinit for service management, we will use the `systemctl` command instead of the `/etc/init.d` scripts to restart the services throughout this book, as follows:

```
$ systemctl restart network.service # Restart the network service
```

You can verify that the previous changes have taken effect using the following command:

```
$ systemctl status network.service # Display the status of the network service
```

You can verify that the expected changes have been correctly applied with the following command:

```
$ ip addr | grep 'inet' ''# Display the IP addresses
```

```
[root@node01 ~]# systemctl restart network.service
[root@node01 ~]# systemctl status network.service
network.service - LSB: Bring up/down networking
   Loaded: loaded (/etc/rc.d/init.d/network)
   Active: active (exited) since Mon 2015-01-26 11:27:33 EST; 6s ago
  Process: 11691 ExecStop=/etc/rc.d/init.d/network stop (code=exited, status=0/SUCCESS)
  Process: 11858 ExecStart=/etc/rc.d/init.d/network start (code=exited, status=0/SUCCESS)

Jan 26 11:27:33 node01 network[11858]: Bringing up loopback interface:  Could not load file '/etc/sy
Jan 26 11:27:33 node01 network[11858]: Could not load file '/etc/sysconfig/network-scripts/ifcfg-lo'
Jan 26 11:27:33 node01 network[11858]: Could not load file '/etc/sysconfig/network-scripts/ifcfg-lo'
Jan 26 11:27:33 node01 network[11858]: Could not load file '/etc/sysconfig/network-scripts/ifcfg-lo'
Jan 26 11:27:33 node01 network[11858]: [  OK  ]
Jan 26 11:27:33 node01 network[11858]: Bringing up interface enp0s3:  Connection successfully activa
Jan 26 11:27:33 node01 network[11858]: [  OK  ]
Jan 26 11:27:33 node01 systemd[1]: Started LSB: Bring up/down networking.
Hint: Some lines were ellipsized, use -l to show in full.
[root@node01 ~]# ip addr | grep inet
    inet 127.0.0.1/8 scope host lo
    inet6 ::1/128 scope host
    inet 192.168.0.2/24 brd 192.168.0.255 scope global enp0s3
    inet6 fe80::a00:27ff:fec8:c2be/64 scope link
[root@node01 ~]#
```

You can disregard all error messages related to the loopback interface as shown in the preceding screenshot. However, you will need to examine carefully any error messages related to `enp0s3`, if any, and get them resolved in order to proceed further.

The second interface will be called `enp0sX`, where X is typically 8, as it is in our case. You can verify this with the following command, as shown in the following screenshot:

```
$ ip link show
```

```
[root@node01 ~]# ip link show
1: lo: <LOOPBACK,UP,LOWER_UP> mtu 65536 qdisc noqueue state UNKNOWN mode DEFAULT
    link/loopback 00:00:00:00:00:00 brd 00:00:00:00:00:00
2: enp0s3: <BROADCAST,MULTICAST,UP,LOWER_UP> mtu 1500 qdisc pfifo_fast state UP mode DEFAULT qlen 1000
    link/ether 08:00:27:c8:c2:be brd ff:ff:ff:ff:ff:ff
3: enp0s8: <BROADCAST,MULTICAST,UP,LOWER_UP> mtu 1500 qdisc pfifo_fast state UP mode DEFAULT qlen 1000
    link/ether 08:00:27:5f:fc:3d brd ff:ff:ff:ff:ff:ff
[root@node01 ~]#
```

As for the configuration file of `enp0s8`, you can safely create it copying the contents of `ifcfg-enp0s3`. Do not forget, however, to change the hardware (MAC) address as returned by the information on the NIC by the `ip link show enp0s8` command and leave the IP address field blank now, using the following command:

```
ip link show enp0s8
```
```
cp /etc/sysconfig/network-scripts/ifcfg-enp0s3 /etc/sysconfig/network-scripts/ifcfg-enp0s8
```

Next, restart the network service as explained earlier.

Note that you will also need to set up at least a basic DNS resolution method. Considering that we will set up a cluster with two nodes only, we will use `/etc/hosts` in both hosts for this purpose.

Edit `/etc/hosts` with the following content:

```
192.168.0.2    node01
192.168.0.3    node02
192.168.0.1    gateway
```

Once you have set up both nodes as explained in the following sections, at this point and before proceeding further, you can perform a ping as a basic test for connectivity between the two hosts to ensure that they are reachable from each other.

To begin, execute in `node01`:

```
$ ping -c 4 node02
```

Next, do the same in `node02`:

```
$ ping -c 4 node01
```

Installing the packages required for clustering

Once we have finished installing the operating system and configuring the basic network infrastructure, we are ready to install the packages that will provide the clustering functionality to each node. Let's emphasize here that without these core components, our two nodes would become simple standalone servers that would not be able to support each other in the event of a system crash or another major issue in one of them.

Key software components

Each node will need the following software components in order to work as a member of the cluster. These packages are fully supported in CentOS 7 as part of a cluster setup, as opposed to other alternatives that have been deprecated:

- **Pacemaker**: This is a cluster resource manager that runs scripts at boot time, when individual nodes go up or down or when related resources fail. In addition, it can be configured to periodically check the health status of each cluster member. In other words, pacemaker will be in charge of starting and stopping services (such as a web or database server, to name a classic example) and will implement the logic to ensure that all of the necessary services are running in only one location at the same time in order to avoid data failure or corruption.
- **Corosync**: This is a messaging service that will provide a communication channel between nodes. As you can guess, corosync is essential for pacemaker to perform its job.
- **PCS**: This is a corosync and pacemaker configuration tool that will allow you to easily view, modify, and create pacemaker-based clusters. This is not strictly necessary but rather optional. We choose to install it because it will come in handy at a later stage.

To install the three preceding software packages, run the following command:

```
$ yum update && yum install pacemaker corosync pcs
```

Yum will update all the installed packages to their most recent version in order to better satisfy dependencies, and it will then proceed with the actual installation.

In addition to installing the preceding packages, we also need to enable `iptables`, as the default firewall for CentOS 7 is `firewalld`. We choose `iptables` over `firewalld` because its use is far more extended, and there is a chance that you will be familiar with it compared with the relatively new `firewalld`. We will install the necessary packages here and leave the configuration for the next chapter.

In order to manage `iptables` via systemd utilities, you will need to install (if it is not already installed) the `iptables-services` package using the following command:

```
yum update && yum install iptables-services
```

Now, you can stop and disable `firewalld` using the following commands:

```
systemctl stop firewalld.service
systemctl disable firewalld.service
```

Next, enable `iptables` to both initialize on boot and start during the current session:

```
systemctl enable iptables.service
systemctl start iptables.service
```

You can refer to the following screenshot for a step-by-step example of this process:

```
[root@node01 ~]# systemctl stop firewalld.service
[root@node01 ~]# systemctl disable firewalld.service
rm '/etc/systemd/system/dbus-org.fedoraproject.FirewallD1.service'
rm '/etc/systemd/system/basic.target.wants/firewalld.service'
[root@node01 ~]# systemctl enable iptables
ln -s '/usr/lib/systemd/system/iptables.service' '/etc/systemd/system/basic.target.wants/iptables.service'
[root@node01 ~]# systemctl start iptables
[root@node01 ~]# systemctl status iptables
iptables.service - IPv4 firewall with iptables
   Loaded: loaded (/usr/lib/systemd/system/iptables.service; enabled)
   Active: active (exited) since Mon 2015-01-26 14:59:35 EST; 8s ago
  Process: 14689 ExecStart=/usr/libexec/iptables/iptables.init start (code=exited, status=0/SUCCESS)
 Main PID: 14689 (code=exited, status=0/SUCCESS)

Jan 26 14:59:35 node01 systemd[1]: Starting IPv4 firewall with iptables...
Jan 26 14:59:35 node01 iptables.init[14689]: iptables: Applying firewall rules: [  OK  ]
Jan 26 14:59:35 node01 systemd[1]: Started IPv4 firewall with iptables.
[root@node01 ~]#
```

Once the installation of the first node (`node01`) has been completed successfully, clone the first node following the outline in section 1.13 of `Virtualbox manual` (`Cloning virtual machines`). Once you're done cloning the virtual machine, add the following minor changes to the second virtual machine:

- Name the machine `node02`. When you start this newly created virtual machine, its hostname will still be set to `node01`. To change it, issue the following command and then reboot the machine to apply it:

  ```
  $ hostnamectl set-hostname node02
  $ systemctl reboot
  ```

- In the configuration file for `enp0s3` in `node02`, enter `192.168.0.3` as the IP address and the right `HWADDR` address.
- Ensure that both the virtual machines are running and that each node can ping the other and the gateway, as shown in the next two screenshots.

First, we will ping `node02` and gateway from `node01`, and we will see the following output:

```
[root@node01 ~]# ping -c 4 node02
PING node02 (192.168.0.3) 56(84) bytes of data.
64 bytes from node02 (192.168.0.3): icmp_seq=1 ttl=64 time=0.638 ms
64 bytes from node02 (192.168.0.3): icmp_seq=2 ttl=64 time=0.811 ms
64 bytes from node02 (192.168.0.3): icmp_seq=3 ttl=64 time=0.708 ms
64 bytes from node02 (192.168.0.3): icmp_seq=4 ttl=64 time=0.887 ms

--- node02 ping statistics ---
4 packets transmitted, 4 received, 0% packet loss, time 3003ms
rtt min/avg/max/mdev = 0.638/0.761/0.887/0.095 ms
[root@node01 ~]# ping -c 4 gateway
PING gateway (192.168.0.1) 56(84) bytes of data.
64 bytes from gateway (192.168.0.1): icmp_seq=1 ttl=64 time=0.568 ms
64 bytes from gateway (192.168.0.1): icmp_seq=2 ttl=64 time=0.870 ms
64 bytes from gateway (192.168.0.1): icmp_seq=3 ttl=64 time=0.730 ms
64 bytes from gateway (192.168.0.1): icmp_seq=4 ttl=64 time=1.00 ms

--- gateway ping statistics ---
4 packets transmitted, 4 received, 0% packet loss, time 3004ms
rtt min/avg/max/mdev = 0.568/0.793/1.007/0.166 ms
[root@node01 ~]#
```

Then, we will ping `node01` and gateway from `node02`:

```
[root@node02 ~]# ping -c 4 node01
PING node01 (192.168.0.2) 56(84) bytes of data.
64 bytes from node01 (192.168.0.2): icmp_seq=1 ttl=64 time=0.699 ms
64 bytes from node01 (192.168.0.2): icmp_seq=2 ttl=64 time=0.863 ms
64 bytes from node01 (192.168.0.2): icmp_seq=3 ttl=64 time=0.903 ms
64 bytes from node01 (192.168.0.2): icmp_seq=4 ttl=64 time=0.797 ms

--- node01 ping statistics ---
4 packets transmitted, 4 received, 0% packet loss, time 3003ms
rtt min/avg/max/mdev = 0.699/0.815/0.903/0.082 ms
[root@node02 ~]# ping -c 4 gateway
PING gateway (192.168.0.1) 56(84) bytes of data.
64 bytes from gateway (192.168.0.1): icmp_seq=1 ttl=64 time=0.738 ms
64 bytes from gateway (192.168.0.1): icmp_seq=2 ttl=64 time=0.800 ms
64 bytes from gateway (192.168.0.1): icmp_seq=3 ttl=64 time=0.841 ms
64 bytes from gateway (192.168.0.1): icmp_seq=4 ttl=64 time=0.974 ms

--- gateway ping statistics ---
4 packets transmitted, 4 received, 0% packet loss, time 3005ms
rtt min/avg/max/mdev = 0.738/0.838/0.974/0.088 ms
[root@node02 ~]#
```

If any of the pings do not return the expected result, as shown in the preceding screenshot, check the network interface configuration in both Virtualbox and in the configuration files, as outlined earlier in this chapter.

Setting up key-based authentication for SSH access

While not strictly required, we will also set up a public key-based authentication for SSH so that we can access each host from the other without entering the accounts password every time we want to access a different node. This feature will come in handy in case, for some reason, we need to perform some system administration task on one of the nodes. Note that you will need to repeat this operation on both nodes.

In order to increase security, we may also enter a passphrase while creating the RSA key, which is shown in the following screenshot. This step is optional and you can omit it if you want. In fact, I advise you to leave it empty in order to make things easier down the road, but it's up to you.

Run the following command in order to create a RSA key:

```
$ ssh-keygen -t rsa
```

```
[root@node01 ~]# ssh-keygen -t rsa
Generating public/private rsa key pair.
Enter file in which to save the key (/root/.ssh/id_rsa):
Created directory '/root/.ssh'.
Enter passphrase (empty for no passphrase):
Enter same passphrase again:
Your identification has been saved in /root/.ssh/id_rsa.
Your public key has been saved in /root/.ssh/id_rsa.pub.
The key fingerprint is:
3f:ff:f2:5e:79:e4:b6:4e:bc:8a:96:be:3a:97:0d:2e root@node01
The key's randomart image is:
+--[ RSA 2048]----+
|                 |
|                 |
|                 |
|                 |
|        S      . |
|       . . .o. |
|        + = +=|
|       E Oo..o+|
|        .B+o**+ |
+-----------------+
[root@node01 ~]#
```

[14]

To enable passwordless login, we will copy the newly created key to `node02`, and vice versa, as shown in the next two figures, respectively.

```
$ cat .ssh/id_rsa.pub | ssh root@node02 'cat' >> .ssh/authorized_keys'
```

Copy the key from `node01` to `node02`:

```
[root@node01 ~]# cat .ssh/id_rsa.pub | ssh root@node02 'cat >> .ssh/authorized_keys'
The authenticity of host 'node02 (192.168.0.3)' can't be established.
ECDSA key fingerprint is 0f:e4:20:d3:ba:8c:fe:34:ce:c5:b3:15:1b:8f:23:f8.
Are you sure you want to continue connecting (yes/no)? yes
Warning: Permanently added 'node02,192.168.0.3' (ECDSA) to the list of known hosts.
root@node02's password:
[root@node01 ~]#
```

Copy the key from `node02` to `node01`:

```
[root@node02 ~]# cat .ssh/id_rsa.pub | ssh root@node01 'cat >> .ssh/authorized_keys'
The authenticity of host 'node01 (192.168.0.2)' can't be established.
ECDSA key fingerprint is 0f:e4:20:d3:ba:8c:fe:34:ce:c5:b3:15:1b:8f:23:f8.
Are you sure you want to continue connecting (yes/no)? yes
Warning: Permanently added 'node01,192.168.0.2' (ECDSA) to the list of known hosts.
root@node01's password:
[root@node02 ~]#
```

Next, we need to verify that we can connect from each cluster member to the other without a password but with the passphrase we entered previously:

```
[root@node01 ~]# ssh node02
Enter passphrase for key '/root/.ssh/id_rsa':
Last login: Mon Jan 26 20:14:23 2015
[root@node02 ~]#
```

```
[root@node02 ~]# ssh node01
Enter passphrase for key '/root/.ssh/id_rsa':
Last login: Mon Jan 26 20:47:25 2015 from node02
[root@node01 ~]#
```

Finally, if passwordless login is not successful, you may want to ensure that the SSH daemon is running on both hosts:

```
$ systemctl status sshd
```

If it is not running, start it using the following command:

```
$ systemctl start sshd
```

You may want to check the status of the service again after attempting to restart it. If there have been any errors, the output of `systemctl status sshd` will give you indications as to what is wrong with the service and why it is refusing to start properly. Following those directions, you will be able to troubleshoot the problem without much hassle.

Summary

In this chapter, we reviewed how to install the operating system and installed the necessary software components to implement the basic cluster functionality. Ensure that you have installed your nodes, the basic clustering software as outlined earlier in this chapter, and configured the network and SSH access before proceeding with *Chapter 2, Installing Cluster Services and Configuring Network Components*, where we will configure the resource manager, the messaging layer, and the firewall service in order to actually start building our cluster.

2
Installing Cluster Services and Configuring Network Components

In this chapter, you will learn how to set up and configure the basic required network infrastructure and also the clustering components that we installed in the previous chapter.

In addition to this, we will review the basic and important concepts of firewalling and Internet protocols, and we will explain how to add the firewall rules that will allow communication between the nodes and the proper operation of the clustering services on each node.

If your native language is any other than English, you must have taken an English class or taught yourself (as I did) before being able to read this book. The same thing happens when two people who do not speak the same language want to communicate with each other. At least one of them needs to know the language of the other, or the two of them need to agree on a common idiom in order to be able to understand each other.

In networking, the equivalent of languages in the above analogy is called **protocols**. In order to enable data transmission between two machines, there must be a logical way for them to be able to speak to each other. This is at the very heart of the Internet protocol suite, also known as the **Internet model**, which provides a set of communication protocols or rules.

It is precisely this set of protocols that make data transmission possible in networks such as the Internet. Later in this chapter, we will explain the protocols and network ports that participate in the communication inside a cluster.

Configuring and starting clustering services

Having reviewed the key networking concepts that were outlined earlier, we are now ready to start describing the cluster services.

Starting and enabling clustering services

You will recall from the previous chapter that we installed the following clustering components:

- **Pacemaker**: This is the cluster resource manager
- **Corosync**: This is the messaging service
- **PCS**: This is the synchronization and configuration tool

As you can probably guess from the preceding list, these components should run as daemons, a special type of process that runs in the background without the need of direct intervention or control of an administrator. Although we installed the necessary packages in *Chapter 1, Cluster Basics and Installation on CentOS 7*, we did not start the cluster resource manager or the messaging services. So, we now need to start them manually for the first time and enable them to run automatically on startup during the next system boot.

We will start by configuring `pacemaker` and `corosync` first and save PCS for later in this chapter.

As shown in the following screenshot, these daemons (also known as units in systemd-based systems) are inactive when you first boot both nodes (and are not automatically started on reboot) after performing all the tasks outlined in *Chapter 1, Cluster Basics and Installation on CentOS 7*. You can check their current running status using the following commands:

```
systemctl status pacemaker
systemctl status corosync
```

```
[root@node01 ~]# systemctl status pacemaker
pacemaker.service - Pacemaker High Availability Cluster Manager
   Loaded: loaded (/usr/lib/systemd/system/pacemaker.service; disabled)
   Active: inactive (dead)

[root@node01 ~]# systemctl status corosync
corosync.service - Corosync Cluster Engine
   Loaded: loaded (/usr/lib/systemd/system/corosync.service; disabled)
   Active: inactive (dead)

[root@node01 ~]#
```

In order to start corosync and pacemaker on each node and enable both services to start automatically during system boot, first create the corosync configuration file by making a copy of the example file, which came with the installation package. As opposed to the pacemaker and PCS, corosync does not create the configuration file automatically for you:

To create the corosync configuration file, do:

```
cp /etc/corosync/corosync.conf.example /etc/corosync/corosync.conf
```

And then restart and enable the services by running the following commands:

```
systemctl start pacemaker
systemctl enable corosync
systemctl enable pacemaker
```

In the preceding commands, note that we are not starting corosync manually, as it will launch on its own when pacemaker is started. It is important to note that on systemd-based systems, enabling a service is not the same as starting it. A unit may be enabled but not started, or the other way around. As shown in the following code, enabling a service involves creating a symlink to the unit's configuration file, which among other things specifies the actions to be taken on system boot and shutdown.

Perform the following operations on both nodes:

```
[root@node01 ~]# systemctl enable pacemaker
ln -s '/usr/lib/systemd/system/pacemaker.service' '/etc/systemd/system/multi-user.target.wants/pacemaker.service'
[root@node01 ~]# systemctl enable corosync
ln -s '/usr/lib/systemd/system/corosync.service' '/etc/systemd/system/multi-user.target.wants/corosync.service'
[root@node01 ~]#
```

Finally, before we can configure the cluster at a later stage, we need to perform the following steps:

1. Start and enable the PCS daemon (`pcsd`), which will be in charge of keeping the corosync configuration synced on `node01` and `node02`. In order for the `pcsd` daemon to work as expected, corosync and pacemaker must have been started previously. Note that when you use the `systemctl` tool to manage services in a systemd-based system, you can omit the trailing `.service` after the daemon name (or use it if you want, as indicated in *Chapter 1, Cluster Basics and Installation on CentOS 7*). Start and enable the PCS daemon with:

   ```
   systemctl start pcsd
   systemctl enable pcsd
   ```

2. Now set the password for the hacluster Linux account, which was created automatically when PCS was installed. This account is used by the PCS daemon to set up communication between nodes, and is best managed when the password is identical on both nodes. To set the password for hacluster, type the following command and assign the same password on both nodes:

`passwd hacluster`

Troubleshooting

Under normal circumstances, starting pacemaker should start corosync automatically. You can check corosync's status with the `systemctl status corosync` command. If for some reason that is not the case, you can still run the following command to manually start the messaging service:

`systemctl start corosync`

Should any of the preceding commands return an error, running `systemctl -l status unit`, where `unit` is either corosync or pacemaker, will return a detailed status about the respective service.

Here is another useful troubleshooting command:

`journalctl -xn`

This will query the systemd journal (systemd's own log) and return verbose messages about the last events.

Both of these commands will provide helpful information as to what went wrong, and point you in the right direction to solve the problem.

> You can read more about the systemd journal in its man page, *man journalctl*, or in the online version, which is available at http://www.freedesktop.org/software/systemd/man/journalctl.html.

Security fundamentals

At this point, we are ready to discuss network security to only allow the proper network traffic between the nodes. During the initial setup and while performing your first tests, you may want to disable the firewall and SELinux (which is described later in this chapter) and then go through both of them at a later stage—it is up to you depending on your grade of familiarity with them at this point.

Letting in and letting out

After having started and enabled the services mentioned earlier, we are ready to take a closer look at the network processes involved in the cluster configuration and maintenance. With the help of the `netstat` command, a tool included in the `net-tools` package for CentOS 7, we will print the current listening network ports and verify that corosync is running and listening for connections. Before doing so, you will need to install the net-tools package, as it is not included in the minimal CentOS 7 setup, using the following command:

```
yum -y install net-tools && netstat -npltu | grep -i corosync
```

As we can see in the following screenshot, Corosync is listening on the **UDP** ports `5404` and `5405` of the loopback interface (`127.0.0.1`) and on the port `5405` of the multicast address (which is set to `239.255.1.1` by default and provides a logical way to identify this group of nodes):

```
[root@node02 ~]# netstat -npltu | grep -i corosync
udp        0      0 127.0.0.1:5404          0.0.0.0:*                           6259/corosync
udp        0      0 127.0.0.1:5405          0.0.0.0:*                           6259/corosync
udp        0      0 239.255.1.1:5405        0.0.0.0:*                           6259/corosync
[root@node02 ~]#
```

> **User Datagram Protocol** (UDP) is one of the core members of the Internet model. This protocol allows applications to send messages (also known as **datagrams**) to hosts in a network in order to set up paths for data transmission without performing full handshakes (or a successful connection between two hosts in a network). Additionally, UDP does not include error checking and correction in a network communication (these checks are performed at the destination application itself).
>
> The **Transmission Control Protocol** (**TCP**) is another core protocol of the Internet model. As opposed to UDP, it provides error, delivery, ordering, and duplicates checking of data streams between computers in a network. Several well-known application layer protocols (such as HTTP, SMTP, and SSH, to name a few) are encapsulated in TCP.
>
> **Internet Group Management Protocol** (**IGMP**) is the communication protocol used by network devices (whether they can be either hosts or routers) to establish multicast data transmissions, which allows one host on the network to send datagrams to several other systems that are interested in receiving the source content.

Installing Cluster Services and Configuring Network Components

Before we proceed further, we will need to allow traffic through the firewall on each node. By default, the ports named in the following list are the default ports where these services will listen after being started, as we previously did. Specifically, in both nodes, we need to perform the following steps:

1. Open the network ports needed by `corosync` (**UDP** ports **5404** and **5405**) and PCS (usually **TCP 2224**) using the following commands:

    ```
    iptables -I INPUT -m state --state NEW -p udp -m multiport --dports 5404,5405 -j ACCEPT
    
    iptables -I INPUT -p tcp -m state --state NEW --dport 2224 -j ACCEPT
    ```

    > Note that the use of `-m` multiport allows you to combine a number of different ports in one rule instead of having to write several rules that are almost identical. This results in fewer rules and easier maintenance of `iptables`.

2. Allow IGMP and multicast traffic using the following commands:

    ```
    iptables -I INPUT -p igmp -j ACCEPT
    iptables -I INPUT -m addrtype --dst-type MULTICAST -j ACCEPT
    ```

3. Change the default `iptables` policy for the `INPUT` chain to `DROP`. Thus, any packet that does not comply with the rules that we just added will be dropped. Note that, as opposed to the `REJECT` policy, `DROP` does not send any response whatsoever to the calling client, just "radio silence" while actively dropping the packets:

    ```
    iptables -P INPUT DROP
    ```

4. After adding the necessary rules, our firewall configuration looks as shown in the following code, where we can clearly see that besides the rules that we added in the two previous steps, there are others that were initialized by default when we started and enabled `iptables`, as explained in *Chapter 1, Cluster Basics and Installation on CentOS 7*. Run the following command to list the firewall rules along with their corresponding numbers:

    ```
    [root@node01 ~]# iptables -L -v --line-numbers
    Chain INPUT (policy DROP 0 packets, 0 bytes)
    num   pkts bytes target     prot opt in     out     source               destination
    1      423 48645 ACCEPT     all  --  any    any     anywhere             anywhere             ADDRTYPE match dst-type MULTICAST
    2        0     0 ACCEPT     igmp --  any    any     anywhere             anywhere
    ```

[22]

Chapter 2

```
3        0       0 ACCEPT     tcp  --  any     any     anywhere
anywhere            state NEW tcp dpt:efi-mg
4     1200    124K ACCEPT     udp  --  any     any     anywhere
anywhere            state NEW multiport dports hpoms-dps-
lstn,netsupport
5       86    7152 ACCEPT     all  --  any     any     anywhere
anywhere            state RELATED,ESTABLISHED
6        0       0 ACCEPT     icmp --  any     any     anywhere
anywhere
7      387   41151 ACCEPT     all  --  lo      any     anywhere
anywhere
8        0       0 ACCEPT     tcp  --  any     any     anywhere
anywhere            state NEW tcp dpt:ssh
9       65   10405 REJECT     all  --  any     any     anywhere
anywhere            reject-with icmp-host-prohibited


Chain FORWARD (policy ACCEPT 0 packets, 0 bytes)
num   pkts bytes target     prot opt in      out     source
destination
1        0       0 REJECT     all  --  any     any     anywhere
anywhere            reject-with icmp-host-prohibited


Chain OUTPUT (policy ACCEPT 1149 packets, 127K bytes)
num   pkts bytes target     prot opt in      out     source
destination
```

5. If the last default rule in the INPUT chain implements a REJECT procedure for non-compliant packets, we will delete it because we already took care of that need by changing the default policy for the chain:

   `iptables -D INPUT [rule number]`

6. Finally, we must save the firewall rules for persistency across boots. As shown in the following screenshot, this consists of saving the changes to `/etc/sysconfig/iptables`:

   `service iptables save`

   ```
   [root@node02 ~]# service iptables save
   iptables: Saving firewall rules to /etc/sysconfig/iptables:[  OK  ]
   [root@node02 ~]#
   ```

Installing Cluster Services and Configuring Network Components

If we inspect the /etc/sysconfig/iptables file with our preferred text editor or pager, we will realize that it presents the same firewall rules in a format that is somewhat easier to read, as shown in the following code:

```
[root@node02 ~]# cat /etc/sysconfig/iptables
# Generated by iptables-save v1.4.21 on Sat Dec  5 10:09:24 2015
*filter
:INPUT DROP [0:0]
:FORWARD ACCEPT [0:0]
:OUTPUT ACCEPT [263:28048]
-A INPUT -m addrtype --dst-type MULTICAST -j ACCEPT
-A INPUT -p igmp -j ACCEPT
-A INPUT -p tcp -m state --state NEW -m tcp --dport 2224 -j ACCEPT
-A INPUT -p udp -m state --state NEW -m multiport --dports 5404,5405 -j ACCEPT
-A INPUT -m state --state RELATED,ESTABLISHED -j ACCEPT
-A INPUT -p icmp -j ACCEPT
-A INPUT -i lo -j ACCEPT
-A INPUT -p tcp -m state --state NEW -m tcp --dport 22 -j ACCEPT
-A INPUT -j REJECT --reject-with icmp-host-prohibited
-A FORWARD -j REJECT --reject-with icmp-host-prohibited
COMMIT
# Completed on Sat Dec  5 10:09:24 2015
```

Next, you will also need to edit the /etc/sysconfig/iptables-config file to indicate that firewall rules should be persistent on system shutdown and reboot. Note that these lines already exist in the file and need to be changed. As a precaution, you may want to back up the existing file before making the change:

`cp /etc/sysconfig/iptables-config /etc/sysconfig/iptables-config.orig`

Now, open /etc/sysconfig/iptables-config with your preferred text editor and ensure that the indicated lines read as follows:

```
IPTABLES_SAVE_ON_STOP="yes"
IPTABLES_SAVE_ON_RESTART="yes"
```

As usual, do not forget to restart iptables (systemctl restart iptables) in order to apply changes.

CentOS 7, just like the previous versions of the distribution, comes with built-in **SELinux (Security Enhanced Linux)** support. This provides native, flexible access control functionality for the operating system based on the kernel itself. You may well be wondering what to do with SELinux policies at this stage. The current settings, which can be displayed with the `sestatus` and `getenforce` commands, and are shown in the following screenshot, will do for the time being:

```
[root@node02 ~]# sestatus
SELinux status:                 enabled
SELinuxfs mount:                /sys/fs/selinux
SELinux root directory:         /etc/selinux
Loaded policy name:             targeted
Current mode:                   enforcing
Mode from config file:          enforcing
Policy MLS status:              enabled
Policy deny_unknown status:     allowed
Max kernel policy version:      28
[root@node02 ~]# getenforce
Enforcing
[root@node02 ~]#
```

In simple terms, we will leave the default mode set to `enforcing` for security purposes. This should not cause any issues further down the road, but if it does, feel free to set the mode to `permissive` with the following command:

`setenforce 0`

The preceding command will enable warnings and log errors to help you troubleshoot issues while the server is still running. In case you need to troubleshoot issues and you suspect that SELinux may be causing them, you should look in `/var/log/audit/audit.log`. SELinux log messages, which are labeled with the AVC keyword, are written to that file via `auditd`, the Linux auditing system, which is started by default. Otherwise, these messages are written to `/var/log/messages`.

Now, before you tackle the next heading, don't forget to repeat the same operations and save the changes on the other node as well!

Getting acquainted with PCS

We are getting closer to actually setting up the cluster. Before diving into that task, we need to become familiar with PCS—the core component of our cluster—so to speak, which will be used to control and configure pacemaker and corosync. To begin doing that, we can just run PCS without arguments, as follows:

`pcs`

Installing Cluster Services and Configuring Network Components

This returns the output shown in the following screenshot, which provides a short explanation of each option and command available in PCS:

```
[root@node01 ~]# pcs

Usage: pcs [-f file] [-h] [commands]...
Control and configure pacemaker and corosync.

Options:
    -h, --help  Display usage and exit
    -f file     Perform actions on file instead of active CIB
    --debug     Print all network traffic and external commands run
    --version   Print pcs version information

Commands:
    cluster     Configure cluster options and nodes
    resource    Manage cluster resources
    stonith     Configure fence devices
    constraint  Set resource constraints
    property    Set pacemaker properties
    status      View cluster status
    config      Print full cluster configuration

[root@node01 ~]#
```

We are interested in the **Commands** section, where the actual categories of clustering that can be managed through this tool are listed, along with a brief description of their usage. Each of them supports several capabilities, which can be shown by appending the word **help** to `pcs [category]`. For example, let's' see the functionality that is provided by the `cluster` command (which by the way, we will use shortly):

```
pcs cluster help
Usage: pcs cluster [commands]...
Configure cluster for use with pacemaker

Commands:
    auth [node] [...] [-u username] [-p password] [--force] [--local]
        Authenticate pcs to pcsd on nodes specified, or on all nodes
        configured in corosync.conf if no nodes are specified (authorization
        tokens are stored in ~/.pcs/tokens or /var/lib/pcsd/tokens for root).
        By default all nodes are also authenticated to each other, using
        --local only authenticates the local node (and does not authenticate
        the remote nodes with each other). Using --force forces
        re-authentication to occur.

    setup [--start] [--local] [--enable] --name <cluster name>
<node1[,node1-altaddr]>
```

```
                [node2[,node2-altaddr]] [..] [--transport <udpu|udp>] [--rrpmode
active|passive]
            [--addr0 <addr/net> [[[--mcast0 <address>] [--mcastport0 <port>]
                        [--ttl0 <ttl>]] | [--broadcast0]]
            [--addr1 <addr/net> [[[--mcast1 <address>] [--mcastport1 <port>]
                        [--ttl1 <ttl>]] | [--broadcast1]]]]
            [--wait_for_all=<0|1>] [--auto_tie_breaker=<0|1>]
            [--last_man_standing=<0|1> [--last_man_standing_window=<time in
ms>]]
            [--ipv6] [--token <timeout>] [--join <timeout>]
            [--consensus <timeout>] [--miss_count_const <count>]
            [--fail_recv_const <failures>]
    Configure corosync and sync configuration out to listed nodes
    --local will only perform changes on the local node
    --start will also start the cluster on the specified nodes
    --enable will enable corosync and pacemaker on node startup
    --transport allows specification of corosync transport (default:
udpu)
    The --wait_for_all, --auto_tie_breaker, --last_man_standing,
    --last_man_standing_window options are all documented in corosync's'
    votequorum(5) man page.
    --ipv6 will configure corosync to use ipv6 (instead of ipv4)
    --token <timeout> sets time in milliseconds until a token loss is
        declared after not receiving a token (default 1000 ms)
    --join <timeout> sets time in milliseconds to wait for join mesages
        (default 50 ms)
    --consensus <timeout> sets time in milliseconds to wait for
consensus
        to be achieved before starting a new round of membership
configuration
        (default 1200 ms)
    --miss_count_const <count> sets the maximum number of times on
        receipt of a token a message is checked for retransmission
before
        a retransmission occurs (default 5 messages)
    --fail_recv_const <failures> specifies how many rotations of the
token
        without receiving any messages when messages should be received
        may occur before a new configuration is formed (default 2500
failures)
```

Installing Cluster Services and Configuring Network Components

> Note that the output is truncated for brevity.

You will often find yourself examining the documentation, so you should consider seriously becoming acquainted with the help.

Managing authentication and creating the cluster

We are now ready to authenticate PCS to the `pcsd` service on the nodes specified in the command line. By default, all nodes are authenticated to each other and thus PCS can talk to itself from one cluster member to the rest.

This is precisely where the hacluster user (of which we changed the password earlier) comes in handy, as it is the account that is used for this purpose. The generic syntax for PCS to perform this step in a cluster with N nodes is as follows:

```
pcs cluster auth member1 member 2 ... memberN
```

In our current setup with two nodes, setting up authentication means:

```
pcs cluster auth node01 node02
```

We will be prompted to enter the username and password that will be used for authentication, as discussed earlier, and fortunately for us, this process does not need to be repeated as we can now control the cluster from any of the nodes. This procedure is exemplified in the following screenshot (where we set up the authentication for `pcs` from `node01`), and later when we create the cluster itself issuing the command in `node02`, from where the `/etc/corosync/corosync.conf` file is synchronized to the other node:

```
[root@node01 ~]# pcs cluster auth node01 node02
Username: hacluster
Password:
node01: Authorized
node02: Authorized
[root@node01 ~]#
```

To create the cluster using the specified nodes, type (on one node only, after successfully trying the password as illustrated in the preceding screenshot) the following command:

```
pcs cluster setup --name MyCluster node01 node02
```

Chapter 2

Here, `MyCluster` is the name we have chosen for our cluster (and you may want to change it according to your liking). Next, press *Enter* and verify the output. Note that it is this command that creates the cluster configuration file in `/etc/corosync/corosync.conf` on both nodes.

If you created the `corosync.conf` file using the sample configuration file as instructed earlier in this chapter (in order to start pacemaker and corosync), you will have to use the `--force` option to overwrite that file with the current settings of the newly created cluster:

```
[root@node01 ~]# pcs cluster setup --name MyCluster node01 node02
Error: /etc/corosync/corosync.conf already exists, use --force to overwrite
[root@node01 ~]# pcs cluster setup --name MyCluster node01 node02 --force
Shutting down pacemaker/corosync services...
Redirecting to /bin/systemctl stop  pacemaker.service
Redirecting to /bin/systemctl stop  corosync.service
Killing any remaining services...
Removing all cluster configuration files...
node01: Succeeded
node02: Succeeded
[root@node01 ~]#
```

> If you get the following error message while trying to set up the `pcs` authentication. Ensure that `pcsd` is running (and enabled) on nodeXX, and try again:
> **Error: Unable to communicate with nodeXX**
> (Here, XX is the node number)

At this point, the `/etc/corosync/corosync.conf` file in `node02` should be identical to the same file in `node01`, as can be seen in the output of the following `diff` command, when run from either node. An empty output indicates that the corosync configuration file has been correctly synced from one node to the other:

```
diff /etc/corosync/corosync.conf <(ssh node02 'cat /etc/corosync/corosync.conf')
```

The next step consists of actually starting the cluster by issuing the command (again, on one node only):

```
pcs cluster start --all
```

[29]

Installing Cluster Services and Configuring Network Components

> The command that is used to start the cluster (`pcs cluster start`) deserves further clarification:
>
> ```
> start [--all] [node] [...]
>     Start corosync & pacemaker on specified node(s),
> if a node is not
>     specified then corosync & pacemaker are started
> on the local node.
>     If --all is specified then corosync & pacemaker
> are started on all
>     nodes.
> ```
>
> There will be times when you want to start the cluster on a specific node. In that case, you will name such a node instead of using the `--all` flag.

The output to the preceding command should be as follows:

```
pcs cluster start --all
[root@node01 ~]# pcs cluster start --all
node01: Starting Cluster...
node02: Starting Cluster...
[root@node01 ~]#
```

Once the cluster has been started, you can check its status from any of the nodes (remember that PCS makes it possible for you to manage the cluster from any node):

```
[root@node01 log]# pcs status cluster
Cluster Status:
 Last updated: Sat Dec  5 11:59:14 2015          Last change: Sat Dec  5 11:53:01 2015 by root via cibadmin on node01
 Stack: corosync
 Current DC: node02 (version 1.1.13-a14efad) - partition with quorum
 2 nodes and 0 resources configured
 Online: [ node01 node02 ]
[root@node01 log]#or just pcs status:
[root@node01 log]# pcs status
Cluster name: MyCluster
WARNING: no stonith devices and stonith-enabled is not false
Last updated: Sat Dec  5 11:55:43 2015          Last change: Sat Dec  5 11:53:01 2015 by root via cibadmin on node01
```

```
Stack: corosync
Current DC: node02 (version 1.1.13-a14efad) - partition with quorum
2 nodes and 0 resources configured


Online: [ node01 node02 ]


Full list of resources:



PCSD Status:
  node01: Online
  node02: Online

Daemon Status:
  corosync: active/disabled
  pacemaker: active/disabled
  pcsd: active/enabled
```

> The `pcs status` command provides more detailed information, including the status of services and resources. It is possible that you notice that one of the nodes is OFFLINE, as follows:
>
> Online: [node01]
>
> OFFLINE: [node02]
>
> In this case, ensure that both pacemaker and corosync are enabled (as indicated after the `Daemon status:` line) and started on the node that's marked as OFFLINE, and then perform `pcs status` again.
>
> Another issue you may encounter is having one or more of the nodes in an unclean state. While that is not common, resyncing the nodes by stopping and restarting the cluster on both nodes will fix it:
>
> pcs cluster stop
> pcs cluster start

Installing Cluster Services and Configuring Network Components

The node that is marked as **DC**, that is, **Designated Controller**, is the node where the cluster was originally started and from where the cluster-related commands will be typically issued. If for some reason, the current DC fails, a new designated controller is chosen automatically from the remaining nodes. You can see which node is the current DC with:

```
pcs status | grep -i dc
```

To see the current DC in your cluster, do:

```
[root@node01 ~]# pcs status | grep -i dc
Current DC: node02 (version 1.1.13-a14efad) - partition with quorum
[root@node01 ~]#
```

You will also want to check on each node individually:

The `pcs status nodes` command allows you to view all information about the cluster and its configured resources:

```
[root@node01 ~]# pcs status nodes
Pacemaker Nodes:
Online: node01 node02
Standby:
Offline:
[root@node01 ~]#
```

The `corosync-cmapctl` command is another tool for accessing the cluster's object database, where you will be able to view the properties and configuration of each node. Since the output of `corosync-cmapctl` command is rather lengthy, you may want to filter by a chosen keyword, such as members or cluster_name, for example:

```
[root@node01 ~]# corosync-cmapctl | grep -Ei 'cluster'_name|members'
runtime.totem.pg.mrp.srp.members.1.config_version (u64) = 0
runtime.totem.pg.mrp.srp.members.1.ip (str) = r(0) ip(192.168.0.2)
runtime.totem.pg.mrp.srp.members.1.join_count (u32) = 1
runtime.totem.pg.mrp.srp.members.1.status (str) = joined
runtime.totem.pg.mrp.srp.members.2.config_version (u64) = 0
runtime.totem.pg.mrp.srp.members.2.ip (str) = r(0) ip(192.168.0.3)
runtime.totem.pg.mrp.srp.members.2.join_count (u32) = 1
runtime.totem.pg.mrp.srp.members.2.status (str) = joined
totem.cluster_name (str) = MyCluster
[root@node01 ~]#
```

As you can see, the preceding output allows you to see the name of your cluster, the IP address, and the status of each member.

Setting up a virtual IP for the cluster

As mentioned in *Chapter 1*, *Cluster Basics and Installation on CentOS 7*, since a cluster is by definition a group of computers (which we have been referring to as nodes or members) that work together so that the set is seen as a single system from the outside, we need to ensure that end users and clients see it that way.

For this reason, the last thing that we will do in this chapter is configure a virtual IP, which is the address that external clients will use to connect to our cluster. Note that in an ordinary, non-cluster environment, you can use tools, such as `ifconfig` to configure a virtual IP for your system.

However, in our case, we will use nothing more and nothing less than PCS and perform two operations at once:

- Creating the IPv4 address
- Assigning it to the cluster as a whole

Adding a virtual IP as a cluster resource

Since a virtual IP is what is called a **cluster resource**, we will use `pcs resource help` to look for information on to how to create it. You will need, in advance, to pick an IP address that is not being used in your LAN to assign to the virtual IP resource. After the virtual IP is initialized, you can ping it as usual to confirm its availability.

To create the virtual IP named `virtual_ip` with the address `192.168.0.4/24`, monitored everything 30 seconds on `enp0s3`, run the following command on either node:

```
pcs resource create virtual_ip ocf:heartbeat:IPaddr2 ip=192.168.0.4 cidr_netmask=24 nic=enp0s3 op monitor interval=30s
```

Up to this point, the virtual IP resource will show as stopped in the output of `pcs cluster status` or `pcs status` until a later stage when we will disable STONITH (which is a cluster feature that is explained in the next section).

Viewing the status of the virtual IP

To view the current status of cluster resources use the following command:

`pcs status resources`

In case the newly created virtual IP is not started automatically, you will want to perform a more thorough check, including a verbose output of the configuration used by the running cluster as provided by `crm_verify`, a tool that is part of the pacemaker cluster resource manager:

```
[root@node01 ~]# crm_verify -L -V
   error: unpack_resources:     Resource start-up disabled since no STONITH resources have been defined
   error: unpack_resources:     Either configure some or disable STONITH with the stonith-enabled option
   error: unpack_resources:     NOTE: Clusters with shared data need STONITH to ensure data integrity
Errors found during check: config not valid
[root@node01 ~]#
```

> **STONITH**, an acronym for **Shoot The Other Node In The Head**, represents a cluster feature that prevents nodes in a high-availability cluster from becoming active at the same time, and thus serving the same content.

As the preceding error message indicates, clusters with shared data need STONITH to ensure data integrity. However, we will defer the appropriate discussion for this feature for the next chapter, and we will disable it for the time being in order to be able to show how the virtual IP is started and becomes accessible. On the other hand, when `crm_verify -L -V` does not return any output, it means that the configuration is valid and free from errors.

Go ahead and disable STONITH but keep in mind that we will return to this in the next chapter:

`pcs property set stonith-enabled=false`

Next, check the cluster status again.

The resource should now show as started when you query the cluster status. You can check the resource availability by pinging it:

`ping -c 4 192.168.0.4`

If the ping operation returns a warning that some packets were not delivered to destination, refer to `/var/log/pacemaker.log` or `/var/log/cluster/corosync.log` for information on what could have failed.

Summary

In this chapter, you learned how to set up and configure the basic required network infrastructure and also the clustering components that we installed in *Chapter 1, Cluster Basics and Installation on CentOS 7*. Having reviewed the concepts associated with security, firewalling, and Internet protocols, we were able to add the firewall rules that will allow the communication of each node with each other and the proper operation of the clustering services on each box.

We will use the tools discussed in this article throughout the rest of this book, not only to check on the status of the cluster or the individual nodes, but also as a troubleshooting technique in case things don't go as expected.

3
A Closer Look at High Availability

In this chapter, we will look at the components of a high-availability cluster in greater detail than we were able to do initially during *Chapter 1, Cluster Basics and Installation on CentOS 7*; you may want to review that chapter in order to refresh your memory before proceeding further.

In this chapter, we will cover the following topics:

- Failover — a premier on high availability and performance
- Fencing — isolating the malfunctioning nodes
- Split brain — preparing to avoid inconsistencies
- Quorum — scoring inside your cluster
- Configuring our cluster via PCS GUI

We will set out on this chapter by asking ourselves a few questions about how to achieve high availability, and we will attempt to get our answers as we go along. In the next chapter, we will set up actual real-life examples:

- How can we ensure an automatic failover without the need for human intervention?
- How many nodes are needed in a cluster in order to ensure high availability in several failure scenarios?
- How do we consistently ensure data integrity and high availability when an offline node comes online again?

Overall, clusters can be classified into two main categories. For simplicity, we will use a cluster consisting of two nodes for the following definitions, but the concept can be easily extended to a cluster with a higher number of members:

- **Active/Active (A/A)**: In this type of cluster, all nodes are active at the same time. Thus, they are able to serve requests simultaneously and equally, each with independent workloads. When a failover is necessary, the remaining node is assigned an additional processing load, thus impacting the overall performance of the cluster negatively.
- **Active/Passive (A/P)**: In this type of cluster, there is an active node and a passive node. The former handles all traffic under normal circumstances, while the latter just sits idle waiting to enter the scene during a failover, when it actually takes over the situation by servicing requests using its own resources until the other node comes back online.

As you can infer from the last two paragraphs, an A/P cluster presents a clearly desired advantage over A/A, wherein, in the event of a failover, the same percentage of hardware and software resources is made available to end users. This results in a constant performance level in a transparent way, which is specially desired in database servers, where performance is a critical requirement. On the other hand, A/A clusters usually provide higher availability since at least two servers actively run applications and provide services to end users. In the next chapter, you will notice that we will initially set up an A/P cluster in detail and also provide the overall instructions to convert it into an A/A cluster if you wish to do so at a later stage.

Failover – an introduction to high availability and performance

The failover process can be roughly described as the action of switching, in the event of power or network failure, to an available resource to resume operations with the least downtime as possible, with no downtime being the primary goal of high availability clusters.

In *Chapter 2, Installing Cluster Services and Configuring Network Components*, we configured a simple but essential resource for our purposes: a virtual IP address. You will also recall that in order to start becoming acquainted with PCS—the tool that is used as a frontend to PCS (the configuration manager)—we presented a brief introduction to its basic syntax and usage.

> As in other cases in the Linux ecosystem, the program/protocol/package name is written in caps, while the tool and utility is written in lowercase. Thus, PCS is used to indicate the package name, and it is the command-line utility that is used to manage PCS.

With the `pcs status` command, we will be able to view the current status of the cluster and several important pieces of information, as shown in the following screenshot:

```
[root@node01 ~]# pcs status
Cluster name: MyCluster
Last updated: Fri Mar 20 23:24:57 2015
Last change: Tue Feb 24 17:41:02 2015 via cibadmin on node01
Stack: corosync
Current DC: node02 (2) - partition with quorum
Version: 1.1.10-32.el7_0.1-368c726
2 Nodes configured
1 Resources configured


Online: [ node01 node02 ]

Full list of resources:

 virtual_ip     (ocf::heartbeat:IPaddr2):    Started node01

PCSD Status:
  node01: Online
  node02: Online

Daemon Status:
  corosync: active/enabled
  pacemaker: active/enabled
  pcsd: active/enabled
[root@node01 ~]#
```

The following lines present the cluster resources that are currently available for `MyCluster`:

```
Full list of resources:
virtual_ip      (ocf::heartbeat:IPaddr2):    Started node01
```

As indicated, the virtual IP address (conveniently named `virtual_ip` in *Chapter 2, Installing Cluster Services and Configuring Network Components*) is started on `node01`. Since the virtual IP is a cluster resource, it is to be expected that in case the node fails, an automatic failover of this resource is triggered to `node02`. We will simulate a node going offline due to a real issue by stopping both `corosync` and `pacemaker` on that cluster member.

A Closer Look at High Availability

For our current purposes, this simulation will not entitle shutting down (power off) the node because we want to show something interesting in the output of `pcs status` after stopping `corosync` and `pacemaker` in that node.

> You can also simulate a failover by pausing one of the virtual machines in VirtualBox (select the **VM** option in **Oracle VM VirtualBox Manager** and press *Ctrl + P* or choose **Pause** from the **Machine Menu**), and you can also do it by disabling the networking using the `systemctl disable network` command in that node.

Let's stop `pacemaker` and `corosync` in `node01`:

```
pcs cluster stop node01
```

And run again, but on the other node, that is `node02`, using the following command:

```
pcs status
```

To view the current status of the cluster, its nodes, and resources, which is shown in the following screenshot, you will need to run `pcs status` on the node where the cluster is currently running:

```
[root@node02 ~]# pcs status
Cluster name: MyCluster
Last updated: Fri Mar 20 23:55:39 2015
Last change: Tue Feb 24 17:41:02 2015 via cibadmin on node01
Stack: corosync
Current DC: node02 (2) - partition with quorum
Version: 1.1.10-32.el7_0.1-368c726
2 Nodes configured
1 Resources configured


Online: [ node02 ]
OFFLINE: [ node01 ]

Full list of resources:

 virtual_ip     (ocf::heartbeat:IPaddr2):       Started node02

PCSD Status:
  node01: Online
  node02: Online

Daemon Status:
  corosync: active/enabled
  pacemaker: active/enabled
  pcsd: active/enabled
[root@node02 ~]#
```

There are a few lines from the preceding screenshot that are worth discussing.

The **OFFLINE: [node01]** line indicates that `node01` is offline—as far as the cluster as a whole is concerned—which is what we were expecting after stopping the cluster resource manager and the messaging services in that member. However, the following code indicates that the `pcsd` daemon, the remote configuration interface, is still running on `node01`, which makes it possible to still control `pacemaker` and `corosync` in that node, either locally or remotely from another node:

```
PCSD Status:
  node01: Online
```

Finally, the `virtual_ip    (ocf::heartbeat:IPaddr2):    Started node02` command allows us to see that the failover of the virtual IP from `node01` to `node02` was performed automatically and without errors. If, for some reason, you run into errors while performing the virtual IP address failover, you will want to check the related logs for information as to what could have gone wrong.

For example, let's examine a case where the cluster resource does not have another node to failover to. Picture a scenario where `node02` is offline (either because you paused the **VM** or actually shut it down), and all of a sudden, `node01` goes down as well (remember that we are talking about the clustering services not being available instead of an actual power or network outage). Of course, all of this happens behind the scenes—the only thing that you know right now is that you have users complaining that they cannot access whatever application, resource, or service is being offered from your cluster.

The first thing you may feel inclined to try is to see whether the virtual IP address is pingable from within your network (change the IP address as per your choice while configuring the resource at the end of *Chapter 2, Installing Cluster Services and Configuring Network Components*):

```
ping -c 4 192.168.0.4
```

You will notice that none of the four packets was able to reach its intended destination:

```
PING 192.168.0.4 (192.168.0.4) 56(84) bytes of data.
From 192.168.0.2 icmp_seq=1 Destination Host Unreachable
From 192.168.0.2 icmp_seq=2 Destination Host Unreachable
From 192.168.0.2 icmp_seq=3 Destination Host Unreachable
From 192.168.0.2 icmp_seq=4 Destination Host Unreachable
--- 192.168.0.4 ping statistics ---
4 packets transmitted, 0 received, +4 errors, 100% packet loss, time 3000ms
```

For that reason, go to `node01`, where you first started the resource to check on the node's status:

```
Error: cluster is not currently running on this node
```

A Closer Look at High Availability

Then you see that the cluster is down on `node01`. But wasn't the failover supposed to happen automatically? At this point, you have two options:

- Go to `node02` to check whether the cluster is running there.
- Check the logs on `node01`. Note that this assumes that you shut down `node02` and then `node01`. In any event, you want to check the log in the node that you shut down last.

A brief search for the keyword `virtual_ip` in `/var/log/pacemaker.log` (or whatever name you set for the resource during the last stages of *Chapter 2, Installing Cluster Services and Configuring Network Components*) in `node01` tells you what the problem is. Here is a brief excerpt of the `grep virtual_ip /var/log/pacemaker.log` file:

```
Mar 21 07:52:45 [3839] node01    pengine:    info: native_print:
virtual_ip    (ocf::heartbeat:IPaddr2):    Stopped
Mar 21 07:52:45 [3839] node01    pengine:    info: native_color:
Resource virtual_ip cannot run anywhere
Mar 21 07:52:45 [3839] node01    pengine:    info: LogActions:    Leave
virtual_ip    (Stopped)
```

The first message indicates that `virtual_ip` was stopped on `node01`, and the second message states that it could not be failed over anywhere. The result is that the resource is left as `Stopped` (as outlined in the third message) until it is manually re-enabled from either node in the cluster. However, remember that you need to start the cluster on such a node beforehand:

```
pcs cluster start node01
```

Then, run the following command on `node01`:

```
pcs resource enable virtual_ip
```

A further check on `pcs status` may or may not indicate that the resource is still stopped (it is a good idea to ping the virtual IP address here as well). If `virtual_ip` refuses to start, we can use the following command to obtain verbose information about why this particular resource is not being started properly, and then perform a reset of the cluster resource to make it reload its proper configuration:

```
pcs resource debug-start virtual_ip --full
```

Remember that `pcs` takes an option (not required) and a command as arguments, which may in turn be followed by specific options. In this regard, `pcs cluster stop`, where `cluster` is the command and `stop` represents a specific action of such a command, can be used to shut down `corosync` and `pacemaker` on either the local node, all nodes, or a specific node. In the following extract of `man pcs` you can review the syntax of pcs cluster stop:

```
stop [--all] [node] [...]
```

```
Stop corosync and pacemaker on specified node(s), if a node is not
specified then corosync and pacemaker are stopped on the local node. If
--all is specified then corosync and pacemaker are stopped on all nodes.
```

> Remember that when `corosync` and `pacemaker` are running on both nodes, you can run any PCS command to configure the cluster from any of the nodes. In the event of a severe failure, where `pcsd` becomes unavailable on both nodes, you will have to resort to using SSH authentication from one node to the other to troubleshoot and fix issues.
>
> As it happens in other cases, log files are the best friends of system administrators, and they can play a key role in helping you to find out what the root causes of issues are when they happen. There are three logs that you may want to check once in a while and even as you are performing a failover:
>
> - `/var/log/pacemaker.log`
> - `/var/log/cluster/corosync.log`
> - `/var/log/pcsd/pcsd.log`
>
> In addition, you can also search in the systemd log with `journalctl -xn` and use `grep` to filter a specific word or phrase.

> You can reset the status of a cluster resource with the `pcs resource disable <resource_name>` and `pcs resource enable <resource_name>` commands.

Fencing – isolating the malfunctioning nodes

As the number of nodes in a cluster increases, its availability increases, but so does the chance of one of them failing at some point. This failure event, whether serious or not, suggests that we must secure a way to isolate the malfunctioning node from the cluster in order for it to fully release its processing tasks to the rest of the cluster. Think of what an erratic node can cause in a shared storage cluster—data corruption would inevitably occur. The word malfunctioning, in this context, means not only what it suggests in the typical usage of the English language (something that is not working properly), but also a node, which also includes the resources started on it, whose state cannot be determined by the cluster for whatever reason.

A Closer Look at High Availability

This is where the term fencing comes into play. By definition, cluster fencing is the process of isolating, or separating, a node from using its resources or starting services, which it should not have access to, and from the rest of the nodes as well. One of the ABC rules of computer clustering can thus be formulated as, do not let a malfunctioning node run any cluster resources - fence it in all cases. In line with the last statement, an unresponsive node must be taken offline before another node will take over.

Fencing is performed using a mechanism known as STONITH, which we briefly introduced during the last chapter (in few words, STONITH is a fencing method that is used to isolate a failed node in order to prevent it from causing problems in a cluster). You will recall that we disabled this feature at that point and mentioned that we would revisit the topic here. A quick inspection of the cluster's configuration, as shown in the following screenshot, will confirm that that STONITH is currently disabled:

```
[root@node01 ~]# pcs config
Cluster Name: MyCluster
Corosync Nodes:
 node01 node02
Pacemaker Nodes:
 node01 node02

Resources:
 Resource: virtual_ip (class=ocf provider=heartbeat type=IPaddr2)
  Attributes: ip=192.168.0.4 cidr_netmask=24 nic=enp0s3
  Operations: start interval=0s timeout=20s (virtual_ip-start-timeout-20s)
              stop interval=0s timeout=20s (virtual_ip-stop-timeout-20s)
              monitor interval=30s (virtual_ip-monitor-interval-30s)

Stonith Devices:
Fencing Levels:

Location Constraints:
Ordering Constraints:
Colocation Constraints:

Cluster Properties:
 cluster-infrastructure: corosync
 dc-version: 1.1.10-32.el7_0.1-368c726
 stonith-enabled: false
[root@node01 ~]#
```

> If you run the `pcs config` code, you will be able to view the current configuration for the cluster in detail, which is illustrated in the preceding screenshot.
>
> At the very end, the `stonith-enabled: false` line clearly reminds us that STONITH is disabled in our cluster.
>
> You will want to add `pcs config` to the list of essential commands that you must keep in mind as we move forward with the cluster configuration. It will allow you to inspect, at a quick glance, the settings and resources made available through the cluster.

So, let's begin by re-enabling STONITH:

```
pcs property set stonith-enabled=true
```

Next, check on the configuration again, either with the `pcs config` or `pcs property list` command. For brevity, in the case illustrated in the following screenshot, we use the `pcs property list` command in order to introduce you to yet another useful PCS command. Note how we check on this property before and after re-enabling STONITH:

```
[root@node01 ~]# pcs property list
Cluster Properties:
 cluster-infrastructure: corosync
 dc-version: 1.1.10-32.el7_0.1-368c726
 stonith-enabled: false
[root@node01 ~]# pcs property set stonith-enabled=true
[root@node01 ~]# pcs property list
Cluster Properties:
 cluster-infrastructure: corosync
 dc-version: 1.1.10-32.el7_0.1-368c726
 stonith-enabled: true
[root@node01 ~]#
```

Once we have enabled STONITH in our cluster, it is time to finally set up fencing in our cluster by configuring a STONITH resource (also known as a STONITH device).

Installing and configuring a STONITH device

It is worth noting that a STONITH device is a cluster resource that will be used to bring down a malfunctioning or unresponsive node. Installing the following packages on both nodes will make several STONITH devices available in our cluster. If you are setting up your 2-node cluster with two virtual machines, as suggested early in *Chapter 1, Cluster Basics and Installation on CentOS 7*, install the following packages on both nodes:

```
yum update && yum install fence-agents-all fence-virt
```

Once the installation is complete, you can list all the available agents with the `pcs stonith list` command, as shown in the next screenshot.

A Closer Look at High Availability

Each of the listed devices in the following screenshot are described by several available parameters, which can be shown with `pcs stonith describe agent`, where you must replace `agent` with the corresponding name of the resource. Note that we will use these parameters when we actually configure the STONITH device in a later step. The required parameters are indicated by the word (`required`) at the beginning of the description, use the `pcs stonith describe fence_ilo` command, which returns the following output:

```
Stonith options for: fence_ilo
 ipaddr (required): IP Address or Hostname
 login (required): Login Name
 passwd: Login password or passphrase
 ssl: SSL connection
 notls: Disable TLS negotiation
 ribcl: Force ribcl version to use
 ipport: TCP/UDP port to use for connection with device
 inet4_only: Forces agent to use IPv4 addresses only
 inet6_only: Forces agent to use IPv6 addresses only
 passwd_script: Script to retrieve password
 ssl_secure: SSL connection with verifying fence device's' certificate
 ssl_insecure: SSL connection without verifying fence device's' certificate
 action (required): Fencing Action
 verbose: Verbose mode
 debug: Write debug information to given file
 version: Display version information and exit
 help: Display help and exit
 power_timeout: Test X seconds for status change after ON/OFF
 shell_timeout: Wait X seconds for cmd prompt after issuing command
 login_timeout: Wait X seconds for cmd prompt after login
 power_wait: Wait X seconds after issuing ON/OFF
 delay: Wait X seconds before fencing is started
 retry_on: Count of attempts to retry power on
 stonith-timeout: How long to wait for the STONITH action to complete per a stonith device.
 priority: The priority of the stonith resource. Devices are tried in order of highest priority to lowest.
 pcmk_host_map: A mapping of host names to ports numbers for devices that do not support host names.
```

`pcmk_host_list`: A list of machines controlled by this device (Optional unless pcmk_host_check=static-list).

`pcmk_host_check`: How to determine which machines are controlled by the device.

```
[root@node01 ~]# pcs stonith list
fence_apc - Fence agent for APC over telnet/ssh
fence_apc_snmp - Fence agent for APC over SNMP
fence_bladecenter - Fence agent for IBM BladeCenter
fence_brocade - Fence agent for HP Brocade over telnet/ssh
fence_cisco_mds - Fence agent for Cisco MDS
fence_cisco_ucs - Fence agent for Cisco UCS
fence_drac5 - Fence agent for Dell DRAC CMC/5
fence_eaton_snmp - Fence agent for Eaton over SNMP
fence_eps - Fence agent for ePowerSwitch
fence_hpblade - Fence agent for HP BladeSystem
fence_ibmblade - Fence agent for IBM BladeCenter over SNMP
fence_idrac - Fence agent for IPMI over LAN
fence_ifmib - Fence agent for IF MIB
fence_ilo - Fence agent for HP iLO
fence_ilo2 - Fence agent for HP iLO
fence_ilo3 - Fence agent for IPMI over LAN
fence_ilo4 - Fence agent for IPMI over LAN
fence_ilo_mp - Fence agent for HP iLO MP
fence_imm - Fence agent for IPMI over LAN
fence_intelmodular - Fence agent for Intel Modular
fence_ipdu - Fence agent for iPDU over SNMP
fence_ipmilan - Fence agent for IPMI over LAN
fence_kdump - Fence agent for use with kdump
fence_rhevm - Fence agent for RHEV-M REST API
fence_rsb - I/O Fencing agent for Fujitsu-Siemens RSB
fence_scsi - fence agent for SCSI-3 persistent reservations
fence_virt - Fence agent for virtual machines
fence_vmware_soap - Fence agent for VMWare over SOAP API
fence_wti - Fence agent for WTI
fence_xvm - Fence agent for virtual machines
[root@node01 ~]#
```

Among these parameters, you can see that there is an action (`action`) that should take place when a fencing event is going to happen, a host list that will be controlled by this device (`pcmk_host_list`), and a waiting time (`timeout` or `stonith-timeout`), that is, the time taken to wait for a fencing action to complete. These are essential pieces of information that you will need to take into account while specifying the STONITH options during the creation of the device and setting up your infrastructure.

The next step, which consists of creating the device itself, will largely depend on the hardware device that you have available. For example, if you want to fence a Hewlett-Packard node (such as a Proliant server) with a built-in iLO interface, you would use the `fence_ilo` agent, or if your nodes are sitting on top of VMWare virtualization, you may need to choose `fence_vmware_soap`. Another popular option is Dell with **Dell Remote Access Controller (DRAC)**, for which you would use `fence_drac5`. Unfortunately, as of today, there is no out-of-the-box fencing device available for VirtualBox.

> An **iLO (Integrated Lights Out)** card is a separate interface with a separate network connection and IP address that allows a system administrator to perform certain operations on HP servers remotely via HTTPS. Similar functionality is available in Dell servers with built-in DRACs.

Let's now create a STONITH `fence_ilo` device named `Stonith_1`, which can fence `node01` (although we are showing this example using `node01`, note that this has to be done on a per-node basis):

```
pcs stonith create Stonith_1 fence_ilo pcmk_host_list="""node01"
action=reboot --force
```

The basic syntax to create a fencing device is as follows:

```
pcs stonith create stonith_device_name stonith_device_type stonith_device_options
```

You can view an explained list of `stonith_device_options` with man `stonithd`.

To update the device, use the following command:

```
pcs stonith update stonith_device_name stonith_device_options
```

To delete the device, use the following command:

```
pcs stonith delete stonith_device_name
```

Finally, The `pcs stonith show [stonith_device_name] --full` command will display all the options used for `[stonith_device_name]` or all fencing devices if `[stonith_device_name]` is not specified.

You can then simulate a fencing situation (note that this is done automatically behind the scenes under a real-life event) by killing the `pacemaker` and `corosync` processes with the following commands:

```
pcs cluster stop node01 # Clean stop of the cluster on node_name
pcs stonith fence node01 --off
```

Also, confirm that `node_name` is actually offline using the `pcs stonith confirm node01` command.

Split-brain – preparing to avoid inconsistencies

Up to this point, we have considered a few essential concepts in clustering, leading to the following not completely fictitious scenario—what happens if a cluster is formed by nodes that are located in separate networks and the communication link between them goes down? The same applies when the nodes are in the same network and the link goes down as well. That is, none of the nodes have actually gone offline, but each appears to the other as unavailable. The default behavior would be that each node assumes that the other is down and continues serving whatever resources or applications the cluster was previously running.

So far, so good! Now, let's say the network link comes back online but both nodes still think they are the main cluster member. That is where data corruption—at the worst—or inconsistency—at the best—occur. This is caused by possible changes made to data on either side without having been replicated to the other end.

This is why configuring fencing is so important, as is ensuring redundant communication links between cluster members so that such a **Single Point Of Failure** (**SPOF**) does not end up causing the split-brain situation in our cluster.

As far as the fencing is concerned, only the node that is marked as **Designated Controller** (**DC**) and also has quorum can fence the other nodes and run the applications and resources as master, or active, in our A/P cluster. By doing so, we ensure that the other node will not be allowed to take over resources that may lead to the data inconsistencies described earlier.

Quorum – scoring inside your cluster

In simple terms, the concept of quorum indicates the minimum number of members that are required to be active in order for the cluster, as a whole, to be available. Specifically, a cluster is said to have quorum when the number of active nodes is greater than the total number of nodes divided by two. Another way to express this is that quorum is achieved by at least a simple majority (50% of the total number of nodes + 1).

Although the concept of quorum doesn't prevent a split-brain scenario, it will decide which node (or group of nodes) is dominant and allowed to run the cluster so that when a split-brain situation occurs, only one node (or group of nodes) will be able to run the cluster services.

By default, when the cluster does not have quorum, `pacemaker` will stop all resources altogether so that they will not be started on more nodes than desired. However, a cluster member will still listen for other nodes to reappear on the network, but they will not work as a cluster until the quorum exists again.

You can easily confirm this behavior by stopping the cluster on `node01` and `node02` and then restarting it again. You will notice that `virtual_ip` remains stopped:

```
Full list of resources:
virtual_ip     (ocf::heartbeat:IPaddr2):      Stopped
```

Until you enable it manually using the following command:

```
pcs resource enable virtual_ip
```

For a 2-node cluster, as it is in our case, when we used the `pcs cluster` setup in *Chapter 2, Installing Cluster Services and Configuring Network Components*, the following section was added in `/etc/corosync/corosync.conf` for us:

```
quorum {
provider: corosync_votequorum
two_node: 1
}
```

The `two_node: 1` line tells `corosync` that in a 2-node cluster, one member is enough to hold up the quorum. Thus, even when some people would argue that a 2-node cluster is pointless, our cluster will continue working when at least one of the nodes is online. Perhaps you already noticed while stopping and starting the cluster in one node previously, but it is worth pointing out that when trying to stop one of the members in our 2-node clusters, you will be asked to use the `--force` option:

```
pcs cluster stop node01 --force
```

To display the current list of nodes in the cluster and its individual contributions toward cluster quorum (which is shown in the following figure under **Votes** column), run the `corosync-quorumtool -l` command:

```
[root@node02 ~]# corosync-quorumtool -l

Membership information
----------------------
    Nodeid      Votes Name
         1          1 node01
         2          1 node02 (local)
[root@node02 ~]#
```

In a prospective split-brain situation, as described earlier, and supposing that the cluster is divided into two partitions, the partition with a majority of votes remains available, while the other is fenced automatically by the DC if STONITH has been put in place and properly configured. For example, in a 4-node cluster, quorum is established when at least three cluster nodes are functioning. Otherwise, the cluster no longer has quorum and `pacemaker` will stop the services run by the cluster.

Configuring our cluster with PCS GUI

If you followed the steps outlined in *Chapter 2, Installing Cluster Services and Configuring Network Components*, to enable the Hacluster account for cluster administration, we can also use the PCS GUI, a cluster management web interface, to manage clusters. This includes the ability to add, remove, and edit existing clusters.

To navigate to the PCS web interface, go to `https://<ip_of_one_node>:2224` (note that it's `https` and not `http`), accept the security exceptions, and then log in using the credentials that were previously set for Hacluster, as shown in the following screenshot:

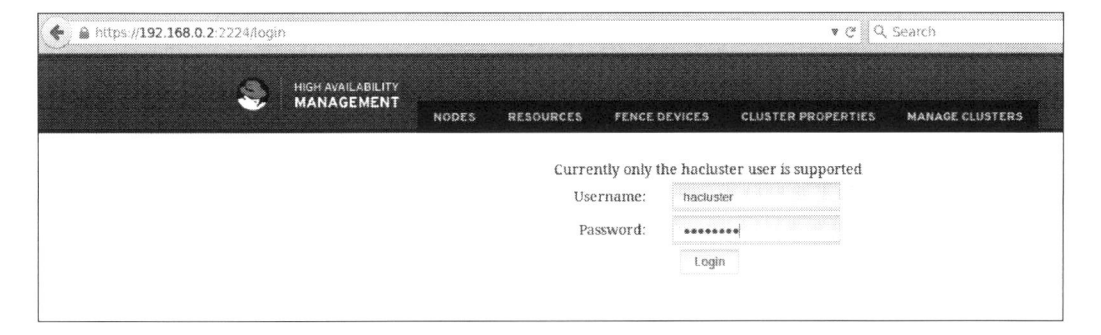

A Closer Look at High Availability

The next screen that you will see (which is as shown in the following screenshot) will present the menus to remove an existing cluster, add an existing cluster, or create a new one. When you click on the **Add Existing** button, you will be prompted to enter the hostname or IP address of a node that currently belongs to an existing cluster that you want to manage using the web UI:

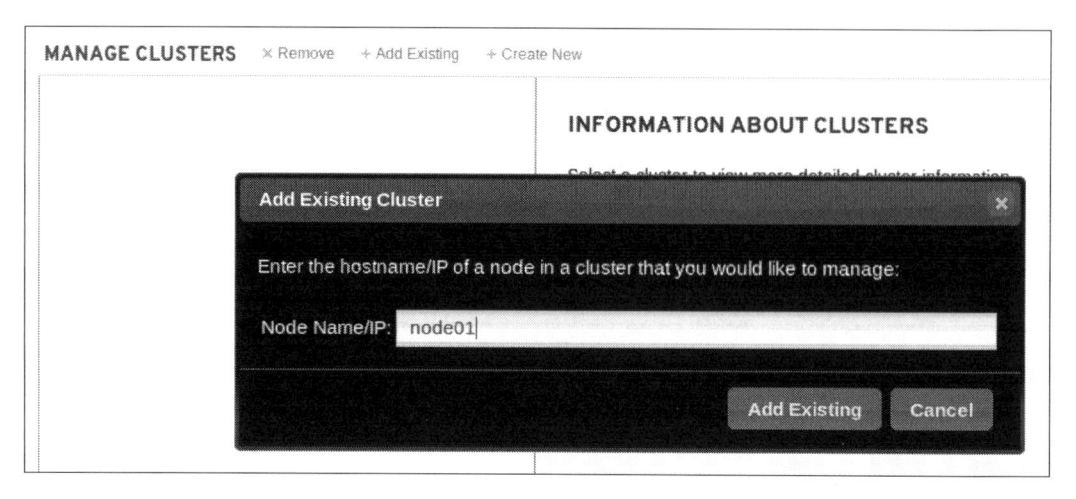

Then, click on the cluster name and feel free to browse through the menu at the top of the following figure, which also serves the purpose of letting us add, remove, or edit the resources that we have been hitherto talking about:

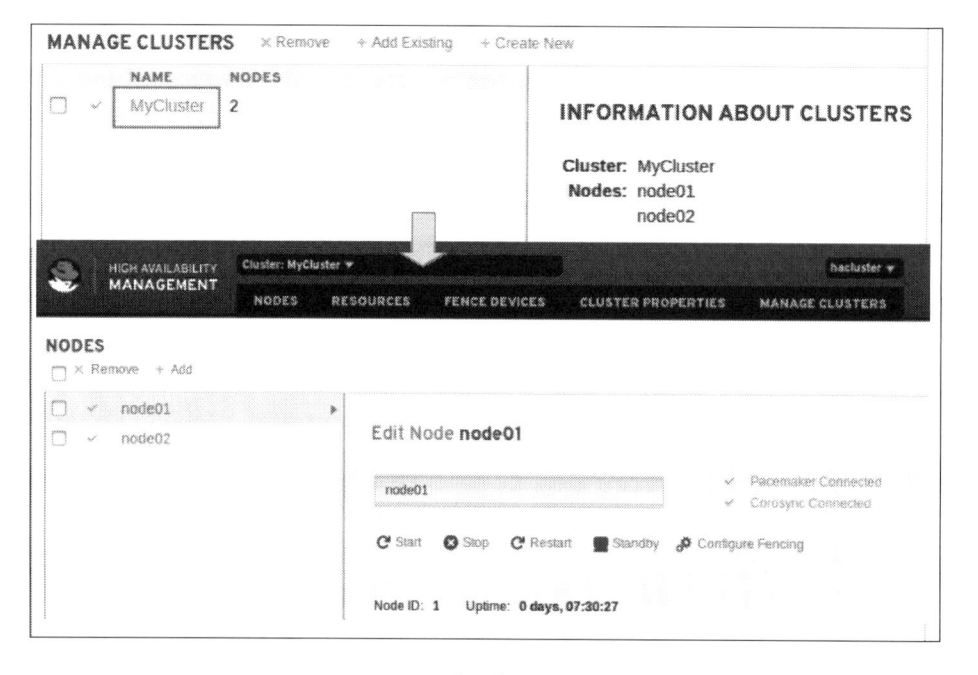

[52]

Summary

In this chapter, we explored situations of node failures and essential techniques for malfunctioning cluster members, along with some essential cluster concepts in greater depth. In addition to this, we saw how to add cluster resources in order to further configure our newly created cluster into a real-world usage case, which we will deal with during the next chapter.

It is also worth reiterating that there are certain hardware components that we have not been able to discuss in detail, such as fencing devices, and you should take note of the fencing agents and devices (as per `pcs stonith list`) and see if any of them applies to the available hardware in your case.

Last but not least, you need to remember that in order to avoid split-brain situations, besides applying thoroughly the concepts outlined in the present chapter, you also need to ensure redundant communication links between the networks where the nodes are located. This will help you prevent a **Single Point Of Failure** (**SPOF**) to potentially cause such an unwanted event.

Real-world Implementations of Clustering

In this chapter, you will learn how to use your cluster in real-life scenarios by deploying a web server and a database server. Before we do this, we will need to review some fundamental concepts related to these key components, configure replicated storage so that files are kept in sync between nodes, and then finally, populate our database with sample data, which we will then query using a simple PHP application.

Since the programming side of things is out of the scope of this book, feel free to use some other programming language of your choice if you want to do so. I have chosen PHP for simplicity. Keep in mind that this book is not aimed at teaching you how to build web-based applications for use in a CentOS 7 cluster, but rather how to use it in order to provide high availability for those applications.

During the course of this chapter, you will notice that we will rely on the concepts introduced and the services configured in previous chapters as we dive into taking advantage of the cluster architecture that we have already put in place.

Setting up storage

When we started discussing the fundamental concepts of clustering, we mentioned that high availability clusters aim, in simple terms, to minimize downtime of services by providing failover capabilities. As we begin the journey of installing a web server and a database server in our cluster, we can't help but wonder how will we synchronize between nodes the content that those services should make available to us. We need to find a way for nodes to share a piece of common storage where data will be saved. If one node fails to provide access to it, the other node will take client requests from then on.

Real-world Implementations of Clustering

In Linux, a common and cost-free method of dealing with this question is an open source technology known as **Distributed Replicated Block Device** (**DRBD**), which makes it possible to mirror or replicate individual storage devices (such as hard disks or partitions) from one node to the other(s) over a network connection. In a somewhat high-level explanation, you can think of the functionality offered by DRBD as a network-based RAID-1. Its basic structure and data flow are illustrated in the following figure:

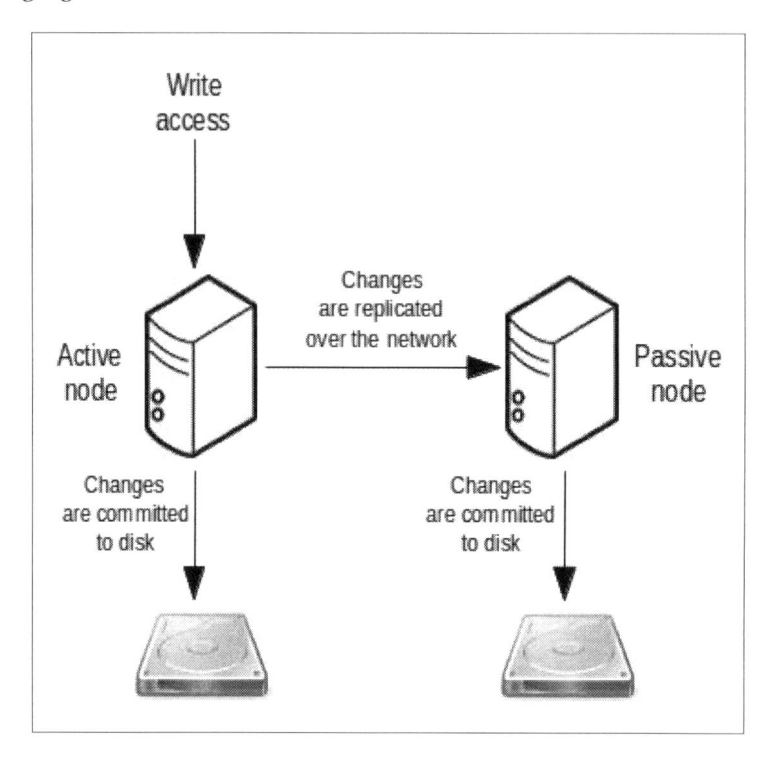

> All replicated data sets, such as a shared storage device, are called a resource in DRBD and should not be confused with a PCS resource, as discussed in previous chapters.

In order to install DRBD, you will need to enable the ELRepo repository on both nodes, because this software package is not distributed through the standard CentOS repositories. Here is a brief explanation of the purpose and contents of the ELRepo repository:

1. The first step consists of importing the GPG key that is used to sign the rpm package, which represents the foundation to the repository. Should you try to install the package using rpm before importing the key, the installation will fail as a security measure.

2. Run the following commands on both nodes:

   ```
   rpm --import https://www.elrepo.org/RPM-GPG-KEY-elrepo.org
   rpm -Uvh http://www.elrepo.org/elrepo-release-7.0-2.el7.elrepo.noarch.rpm
   ```

3. You can verify that ELRepo has been added to your configured repositories with the following command:

   ```
   yum repolist | grep elrepo
   ```

   The output should be similar to the one shown in the following screenshot:

   ```
   [root@node01 ~]# rpm --import https://www.elrepo.org/RPM-GPG-KEY-elrepo.org
   [root@node01 ~]# rpm -Uvh http://www.elrepo.org/elrepo-release-7.0-2.el7.elrepo.noarch.rpm
   Retrieving http://www.elrepo.org/elrepo-release-7.0-2.el7.elrepo.noarch.rpm
   Preparing...                          ################################# [100%]
   Updating / installing...
      1:elrepo-release-7.0-2.el7.elrepo  ################################# [100%]
   [root@node01 ~]# yum repolist | grep elrepo
    * elrepo: reflector.westga.edu
   elrepo          ELRepo.org Community Enterprise Linux Repository - el7    124
   [root@node01 ~]#
   ```

   > Alternatively, you can explicitly disable ELRepo after installing the `rpm` packages that add it to your system and enable it only to install the necessary packages (for precaution, make sure you make a copy of the original repository configuration file first):
   >
   > ```
   > cp /etc/yum.repos.d/elrepo.repo /etc/yum.repos.d/elrepo.repo.ORG
   > sed -i "s/enabled=1/enabled=0/g" /etc/yum.repos.d/elrepo.repo
   > yum --enablerepo elrepo update
   > yum --enablerepo elrepo install -y drbd84-utils kmod-drbd84
   > ```

4. Then, use the following command:

   ```
   yum update && yum install drbd84-utils kmod-drbd84
   ```

   It will install the necessary management utilities, along with the corresponding kernel module for DRBD. Once this process is complete, you will need to check whether the module is loaded, using this command:

   ```
   lsmod | grep -i drbd
   ```

If it is not loaded automatically, you can load the module to the kernel on both nodes, as follows:

```
modprobe drbd
```

> Note that `modprobe` command will take care of loading the kernel module for the time being on your current session. However, in order for it to be loaded during boot, you have to make use of the systemd-modules-load service by creating a file inside `/etc/modules-load.d/` so that the DRBD module is loaded properly each time the system boots:
>
> ```
> echo drbd >/etc/modules-load.d/drbd.conf
> ```

ELRepo repository and DRBD availability

ELRepo is a community repository for Linux distributions that are compatible with Red Hat Enterprise Linux, which CentOS and Scientific Linux are derivatives of. ELRepo has hardware-related packages (especially drivers) as the primary focus in order to enhance or provide functionality that is not present in the current kernel. Thus, by installing the corresponding package, you save yourself from the pain of having to recompile the kernel only to add a certain feature, or having to wait for it to be supported by upstream repositories, or for the feature to be included in a later kernel release. The ELRepo repository is maintained by active members of the related distributions (RHEL, CentOS, and Scientific Linux).

DBRD, as made available by ELRepo, is intended primarily to evaluate and get experience with DRBD on RHEL-based platforms, but is not officially supported by Red Hat and LINBIT, the creators of DRBD. However, following the procedures outlined in this chapter and throughout the rest of this book, you can ensure that all of the necessary functionality will be available in your cluster.

Once we have installed the packages mentioned earlier, we need to allocate the physical space that will be used to store the replicated contents on both servers. With scalability in mind, we will use the **Logical Volume Manager** (**LVM**) technology to create dynamic hard disk partitions that are easily resizable down the road if we need to.

To begin with, we will add a 2 GB hard disk to each node. The purpose of this hard disk is to serve as the underlying filesystem for a PHP application accessed by the Apache web server.

I chose this size because it will be enough to store all the necessary files to be replicated, and because Virtualbox allows you to pick arbitrary sizes for storage disks. If you happen to be using real hardware as you follow along with this book, you may want to choose a different size accordingly.

To add a virtual hard disk to an existing virtual machine in Virtualbox, follow these steps:

1. Turn off the **VM**
2. Right-click on it in Virtualbox's initial screen
3. From the contextual menu, choose **Settings** and then **Storage**
4. Select **Controller: SATA**, and click on **Add hard disk** and then click on **Create new disk**
5. Choose **Virtual Disk Image (VDI)** and **Dynamically Allocated** and proceed to next step
6. Finally, assign a name for the device and choose 2 GB as size

After starting and booting up each node, we should issue the following command in order to identify the newly added disk (the new disk will be, in our case, the one that is not partitioned yet):

```
ls -l /dev | grep -Ei sd[a-z]
```

We will identify the newly added disk with the following command:

```
dmesg | grep sdb
```

Here, /dev/sdb is the new disk ID, as returned by listing the contents of the /dev directory earlier:

```
[root@node02 ~]# dmesg | grep sdb
[    2.484257] sd 3:0:0:0: [sdb] 4194304 512-byte logical blocks: (2.14 GB/2.00 GiB)
[    2.484258] sd 3:0:0:0: [sdb] Write Protect is off
[    2.484258] sd 3:0:0:0: [sdb] Mode Sense: 00 3a 00 00
[    2.484258] sd 3:0:0:0: [sdb] Write cache: enabled, read cache: enabled, doesn't support DPO or FUA
[    2.487361]  sdb: unknown partition table
[    2.498564] sd 3:0:0:0: [sdb] Attached SCSI disk
[root@node02 ~]#
```

Now, let's create a partition on the disk, the corresponding physical volume, a volume group (drbd_vg), and finally, a logical volume (drbd_vol) on top. Make sure you repeat these steps on each node, changing the device (dev/sdX) as needed:

parted /dev/sdb mklabel msdos

parted /dev/sdb mkpart p 0% 100%

pvcreate /dev/sdb1

vgcreate drbd_vg /dev/sdb1

lvcreate -n drbd_vol -l 100%FREE drbd_vg

> You can check the status of the newly created logical volume with lvdisplay /dev/drbd_vg/drbd_vol.

Configuring DRBD

After having successfully created and partitioned our DRBD disks on each node, the main configuration file for DRBD is located in /etc/drbd.conf, which consists only of the following two lines:

```
include "drbd.d/global_common.conf";
include "drbd.d/*.res";
```

Both lines include relative paths, starting at /etc/, of the actual configuration files. In the global_common.conf file, you will find the global settings for your DRBD installation, along with the common section (which defines those settings that should be inherited by every resource) of the DRBD configuration. On the other hand, in the .res files, you will find the specific configuration for each DRBD resource.

We will now rename the existing global_common.conf file as global_common.conf.orig (as a backup copy of the original settings) with the following command:

mv /etc/drbd.d/global_common.conf /etc/drbd.d/global_common.conf.orig

We will then create a new global_common.conf file with the following contents by opening the file with your preferred text editor:

```
global {
 usage-count no;
}
common {
 net {
  protocol C;
 }
}
```

Once you created the preceding file on one node (say, `node01`), you can easily copy it to the another node, as follows:

```
ssh node02 mv /etc/drbd.d/global_common.conf /etc/drbd.d/global_common.conf.orig

scp /etc/drbd.d/global_common.conf node02:/etc/drbd.d/
```

> You should make it a habit to make backup copies of the original configuration files so that you can roll back to previous settings, should something go wrong at any time.

The `usage-count no` line in the global section skips sending a notice to the DRBD team each time a new version of the software is installed in your system. You could change it to `yes` if you want to submit information from your system. Alternatively, you could change it to `ask` if you want to be prompted for a decision each time you do an upgrade. Either way, you should know that they use this information for statistical analysis only, and their reports are always available to the public at http://usage.drbd.org/cgi-bin/show_usage.pl.

The `protocol C` line tells the DRBD resource to use a fully synchronous replication, which means that local write operations on the node that is functioning as primary are considered completed only after both the local and remote disk writes have been confirmed. Thus, if you run into the loss of a single node, that should not lead to any data loss under normal circumstances, unless both nodes (or their storage subsystems) are irreversibly destroyed at the same time.

Next, we will need to create a specific new configuration file file (called /etc/drbd.d/drbd0.res) for our resource, which we will name drbd0, with the following contents (where 192.168.0.2 and 192.168.0.3 are the IP addresses of our two nodes, and 7789 is the port used for communication):

```
resource drbd0 {
    disk /dev/drbd_vg/drbd_vol;
    device /dev/drbd0;
    meta-disk internal;
    on node01 {
            address 192.168.0.2:7789;
    }
    on node02 {
            address 192.168.0.3:7789;
    }
}
```

> You can look up the meaning of each directive (and the rest as well) in the resource configuration file at Linbit's website at http://drbd.linbit.com/users-guide-8.4/.
>
> TCP port 7789 is the typical port number used in most DRBD installations. However, the official documentation states that DRBD (by convention) uses TCP ports from 7788 upwards, with every resource listening on a separate port. In this chapter, since we are dealing with only one resource, we will only use port 7789—both in the only resource configuration file and in the firewall settings on both nodes. It is essential that you remember to open this port in the firewall, because otherwise, the resources will not be able to synchronize later.
>
> To open the 7789 TCP port in the firewall configuration, execute the following commands on both nodes:
>
> `iptables -I INPUT -p tcp -m state --state NEW -m tcp --dport 7789 -j ACCEPT`
>
> `service iptables save`

Again, you can copy this file to the other node, as follows:

`scp /etc/drbd.d/drbd0.res node02:/etc/drbd.d/`

When we installed DRBD earlier, a utility called `drbdadm` was installed as well, which, as you will be able to guess from its name, is intended to be used for the administration of DRBD resources, such as our newly configured volume The first step in starting and bringing a DRBD resource online is to initialize its metadata (you may need to change the resource name if you set a different name in the configuration file previously). Note that the `/var/lib/drbd` directory is needed beforehand. If it was not created previously when you installed DRBD, create it manually before proceeding, using the following lines of code:

`mkdir /var/lib/drbd`

`drbdadm create-md drbd0`

These lines should result in the following output, with the corresponding confirmation message that indicates a successful creation of the metadata for the device:

```
[root@node02 ~]# drbdadm create-md drbd0
initializing activity log
NOT initializing bitmap
Writing meta data...
New drbd meta data block successfully created.
[root@node02 ~]#
```

> The word "metadata" has been defined as data about the data. In the context of DRBD resources, the metadata of a resource consists of several pieces of information about the device and the data that is kept in it. The `drbdadm create-md [drbd resource]` command will return useful debugging information if something does not work as expected.

The next step consists of enabling `drbd0` in order to finish allocating both disk and network resources for its operation:

`drbdadm up drbd0`

You can verify the status of the resource by taking a look at the `/proc` virtual filesystem, which allows you to view the system's resources as the kernel sees them, as you can see in the following screenshot. However, make sure you have followed the instructions outlined earlier on both nodes:

`cat /proc/drbd`

Take a look at the following screenshot:

```
[root@node02 ~]# cat /proc/drbd
version: 8.4.5 (api:1/proto:86-101)
GIT-hash: 1d360bde0e095d495786eaeb2a1ac76888e4db96 build by phil@Build64R7, 2015-03-05 15:53:30
 0: cs:WFConnection ro:Secondary/Unknown ds:Inconsistent/DUnknown C r----s
    ns:0 nr:0 dw:0 dr:0 al:0 bm:0 lo:0 pe:0 ua:0 ap:0 ep:1 wo:f oos:2092956
[root@node02 ~]#
```

Note that the status of the device shows as unknown and inconsistent since we haven't indicated yet which of the DRBD devices (one in each node) will act as a primary device and which one as a secondary device. At this point, given our current scenario where we have set up two DRBD devices from scratch, it does not matter which one you choose to be primary. However, if we had used one device with data already residing in it, it is crucial that you select that one device as the primary resource. Otherwise, you run the serious risk of losing your data.

Run this command in order to mark one device as primary and to perform the initial synchronization. You only need to do this in the node that has the primary resource (in our example, this means `node01`):

`drbdadm primary --force drbd0`

Real-world Implementations of Clustering

As you did earlier, you can check the current status of the synchronization while it's being performed. The cat `/proc/drbd` command displays the creation and synchronization progress of the resource, as shown here:

```
[root@node01 drbd.d]# drbdadm primary --force drbd0
[root@node01 drbd.d]# cat /proc/drbd
version: 8.4.5 (api:1/proto:86-101)
GIT-hash: 1d360bde0e095d495786eaeb2a1ac76888e4db96 build by phil@Build64R7, 2015-03-05 15:53:30
 0: cs:SyncSource ro:Primary/Secondary ds:UpToDate/Inconsistent C r---n-
    ns:1496500 nr:0 dw:0 dr:1497984 al:0 bm:0 lo:0 pe:3 ua:2 ap:0 ep:1 wo:f oos:598940
        [=============>......] sync'ed: 71.5% (598940/2092956)K
        finish: 0:00:14 speed: 40,960 (24,096) K/sec
[root@node01 drbd.d]#
```

Now, with the help of `drbd-overview` command, as its name implies, you can see an overview of the currently configured DRBD resources. In this case, you should see that `node01` is acting as primary and `node02` as secondary, as indicated by running the command on both nodes (which can also be seen in the following screenshot):

In `node01` : the drbd-overview command should return:

`0:drbd0/0   Connected Primary/Secondary UpToDate/UpToDate`

Whereas in `node02` you should see:

`0:drbd0/0   Connected Secondary/Primary UpToDate/UpToDate`

```
[root@node01 ~]# drbd-overview
 0:drbd0/0   Connected Primary/Secondary UpToDate/UpToDate
[root@node01 ~]#

[root@node02 ~]# drbd-overview
 0:drbd0/0   Connected Secondary/Primary UpToDate/UpToDate
[root@node02 ~]#
```

Finally, we need to create a filesystem on `/dev/drbd0` in `node01`. You can choose whatever suits your needs or requirements, if any. `Ext4` is a good choice if you have not decided which one to use. XFS is the default filesystem for CentOS 7 out of the box. However, it is not possible to resize it if we need to do so at a later time, should we run into a more complex setup for the underlying storage needed for the operation of the web and database servers.

Run the following command on the primary node to create an `ext4` filesystem on `/dev/drbd0` and wait until it completes, as shown in the following screenshot:

```
mkfs.ext4 /dev/drbd0
```

```
[root@node01 ~]# ls -l /dev/drbd0
brw-rw----. 1 root disk 147, 0 Apr 15 11:12 /dev/drbd0
[root@node01 ~]# mkfs.ext4 /dev/drbd0
mke2fs 1.42.9 (28-Dec-2013)
Filesystem label=
OS type: Linux
Block size=4096 (log=2)
Fragment size=4096 (log=2)
Stride=0 blocks, Stripe width=0 blocks
130816 inodes, 523239 blocks
26161 blocks (5.00%) reserved for the super user
First data block=0
Maximum filesystem blocks=536870912
16 block groups
32768 blocks per group, 32768 fragments per group
8176 inodes per group
Superblock backups stored on blocks:
        32768, 98304, 163840, 229376, 294912

Allocating group tables: done
Writing inode tables: done
Creating journal (8192 blocks): done
Writing superblocks and filesystem accounting information: done

[root@node01 ~]#
```

Now, your DRBD resource is ready to be used as usual. You can now mount it and start saving files to it. However, we still need to add it as a cluster resource before we can start using it as a highly available and fail-safe component. This is what we will do in the next section.

It is very important that you create the filesystem on the resource from `node01`, our primary node. Otherwise, you will run into a mounting issue that is caused when you try to add a filesystem from a node that is not the primary member of the cluster.

Adding DRBD as a PCS cluster resource

You will recall how in *Chapter 2, Installing Cluster Services and Configuring Network Components*, we added a virtual IP address to the cluster. Now, it's time to do the same with the DRBD resource that we have just created and configured.

Before doing that, however, we must point out that one of the most distinguishing features of the PCS command-line tool that we first introduced back in *Chapter 2, Installing Cluster Services and Configuring Network Components*, is its ability to save the current cluster configuration to a file, to which you can add further settings using command-line tools. Then, you can use the resulting file to update the running cluster configuration.

To retrieve the cluster configuration from the **Cluster Information Base** (**CIB**) and save it to a file named `drbd0_conf` in the current working directory, use the following command to make sure you started the cluster first:

```
pcs cluster start --all
```

Then save the cluster configuration to the file mentioned earlier (`drbd0_conf` will be created automatically):

```
pcs cluster cib drbd0_conf
```

Next, we will add the DRBD device as a PCS cluster resource. Note the `-f` switch, which indicates that changes resulting from the following command should be appended to the `drbd0_conf` file. The following command must be executed from the same directory as the previous command (meaning the directory where the `drbd0_conf` file is located):

```
pcs -f drbd0_conf resource create web_drbd ocf:linbit:drbd drbd_resource=drbd0 op monitor interval=60s
```

Finally, we need to make sure that the resource will run on both nodes simultaneously by adding a clone resource (a special type of resource that should be active on multiple hosts at the same time) for that purpose:

```
pcs -f drbd0_conf resource master web_drbd_clone web_drbd master-max=1 master-node-max=1 clone-max=2 clone-node-max=1 notify=true
```

At this point, we can update the cluster configuration using the `drbd0_conf` file. However, a quick inspection of the cluster status and its resources will allow us to better visualize the changes if we run `pcs status` command before and after updating the global configuration, in that order:

```
pcs status

pcs cluster cib-push drbd0_conf
```

The last command should result in the following message if the update was successful:

`CIB updated`

Now, let's check the current cluster configuration again:

`pcs status`

In the case the last PCS status indicates some failure event (most likely related to SELinux policies and less likely with regular file permissions), you should inspect the `/var/log/audit/audit.log` file to start your troubleshooting. Lines starting with AVC will point out the places where you need to look first. Here is an example:

```
type=AVC msg=audit(1429116572.153:295): avc:  denied  { read write } for pid=24192 comm="drbdsetup-84" name="drbd-147-0" dev="tmpfs" ino=20373 scontext=system_u:system_r:drbd_t:s0 tcontext=unconfined_u:object_r:var_lock_t:s0 tclass=file
```

The preceding error message seems to indicate that SELinux is denying the `drbdsetup-84` executable read/write access to the temporary `tmpfs` filesystem. Its corresponding denied system call supports this theory:

```
type=SYSCALL msg=audit(1429116572.153:295): arch=c000003e syscall=2 success=no exit=-13 a0=125e080 a1=42 a2=180 a3=7fff42b39f80 items=0 ppid=24191 pid=24192 auid=4294967295 uid=0 gid=0 euid=0 suid=0 fsuid=0 egid=0 sgid=0 fsgid=0 tty=(none) ses=4294967295 comm="drbdsetup-84" exe="/usr/lib/drbd/drbdsetup-84" subj=system_u:system_r:drbd_t:s0 key=(null)
```

> NSA Security-Enhanced Linux (SELinux) is an implementation of a flexible mandatory access control architecture in Linux. You can disable it to perform the following steps (but it is strongly recommended that you don't) if you experience several issues with it at first. If you choose to disable SELinux by editing `/etc/sysconfig/selinux`, do not forget to clean the resource error count with `pcs resource cleanup [resource_id]`, where `resource_id` is the name of the resource as returned by `pcs resource show`.

To clear all doubts, install the `policycoreutils-python` package (which contains the management tools used to manage an SELinux environment):

`yum update && yum install policycoreutils-python`

Use the `audit2allow` utility included in it to view the reason of access denied in human-readable form and then generate an SELinux policy-allow rule based on logs of denied operations. The following command will output the last line in the `audit.log` file where the word AVC appears and then pipe it to `audit2allow` to produce the result in human-readable form:

`cat /var/log/audit/audit.log | grep AVC | tail -1 | audit2allow -w -a`

As shown in the following screenshot, we can confirm that access was denied due to a missing type enforcement rule:

```
[root@node01 ~]# cat /var/log/audit/audit.log | grep AVC |tail -1 | audit2allow -w -a
type=AVC msg=audit(1429116572.153:295): avc:  denied  { read write } for  pid=24192 comm="drbdset
m_r:drbd_t:s0 tcontext=unconfined_u:object_r:var_lock_t:s0 tclass=file
        Was caused by:
                Missing type enforcement (TE) allow rule.

                You can use audit2allow to generate a loadable module to allow this access.

[root@node01 ~]#
```

Now that we know what is causing the problem, let's create a policy package in order to implement the necessary type enforcement rule into a module whose name is specified in the command line:

`cat /var/log/audit/audit.log | grep AVC | tail -1 | audit2allow -a -M drbd0_access_0`

If you do `ls -l` in your current working directory, you will find that the preceding command created a type enforcement file (`drbd_access_0.te`) and compiled it into a policy package (`drbd_access_0.pp`), which you will need to activate with the following command:

`semodule -i drbd0_access_0.pp`

The preceding command can take about a minute to complete, so do not worry if this is the case for you, as you can see in the following screenshot, no output means a successful operation:

```
[root@node01 ~]# cat /var/log/audit/audit.log | grep AVC | tail -1 | audit2allow -a -M drbd0_access_0
******************** IMPORTANT ***********************
To make this policy package active, execute:

semodule -i drbd0_access_0.pp

[root@node01 ~]# semodule -i drbd0_access_0.pp
[root@node01 ~]#
```

Now, we need to copy the module to `node02` and install it there. This is one of the reasons why we set up key-based authentication between nodes in *Chapter 1, Cluster Basics and Installation on CentOS 7*:

```
scp drbd0_access_0.pp node02:~
```

Then, run the following command in `node02`:

```
semodule -i drbd0_access_0.pp
```

Alternatively, you can execute the following command in `node01`:

```
ssh node02 semodule -i drbd0_access_0.pp
```

In addition, the SELinux `daemons_enable_cluster_mode` policy should be set to true on both nodes:

```
setsebool -P daemons_enable_cluster_mode 1
```

Then, you may need to repeat this process more than once if the output of `pcs status` shows further errors. If you find that you have to repeat it several times, you may want to consider setting SELinux to permissive so that it will still issue warnings instead of blocking the cluster resource. Then, you can continue with the setup for the time being and debug later.

We can see that both nodes are online, and the cluster resources are properly started, as shown here:

```
[root@node01 ~]# pcs status
Cluster name: MyCluster
Last updated: Wed Apr 15 16:30:21 2015
Last change: Wed Apr 15 16:17:31 2015 via crm_attribute on node02
Stack: corosync
Current DC: node01 (1) - partition with quorum
Version: 1.1.12-a14efad
2 Nodes configured
3 Resources configured


Online: [ node01 node02 ]

Full list of resources:

 virtual_ip     (ocf::heartbeat:IPaddr2):       Started node01
 Master/Slave Set: web_drbd_clone [web_drbd]
     Masters: [ node01 ]
     Slaves: [ node02 ]

PCSD Status:
  node01: Online
  node02: Online

Daemon Status:
  corosync: active/enabled
  pacemaker: active/enabled
  pcsd: active/enabled
```

Now, let's give DRBD a rest for a brief moment, and let's focus on the installation of the web and database servers. Note that we will also revisit this topic in *Chapter 5*, *Monitoring the Cluster Health*, where we will simulate and troubleshoot issues. Note that if you reboot a node or both of them, nodes may detect a split-brain situation at this point, which we will fix manually (as that is the method that is recommended by LINBIT) later during the next chapter, when we troubleshoot the most common issues that may come up during the cluster operation.

Installing the web and database servers

As of the time of writing this book, the Apache HTTP server (or just Apache for short) remains the world's most widely used web server and is often used within what is called a **LAMP stack**. In this stack, a Linux distribution is used as the operating system, Apache as the web server, MySQL/MariaDB as the database server, and PHP as the server-side programming language for applications. Each one of these components is free, and these technologies are widely spread and thus easy to learn/get help on.

To install the Apache and MariaDB (a free and open source fork of MySQL) servers, run the following commands on each node. Note that this will install PHP as well:

```
yum update && yum install httpd mariadb mariadb-server php
```

Upon successful installation, we will proceed as we did earlier. To begin, let's enable and start the web server on both nodes:

```
systemctl enable httpd
systemctl start httpd
```

Don't forget to make sure that Apache is running:

```
systemctl status httpd
```

Allow traffic through TCP port 80 in the firewall:

```
iptables -I INPUT -p tcp -m state --state NEW -m tcp --dport 80 -j ACCEPT
service iptables save
```

At this point, you can fire up a web browser and point it to the individual IP addresses of the nodes (remember that we haven't added Apache as a cluster resource, and thus, we can't access the web server on the virtual IP that is common to both nodes). You should see Apache's welcome page, as shown in the following figure, where we can see that web server is running correctly on `node02` (`192.168.0.3` as per our initial setup):

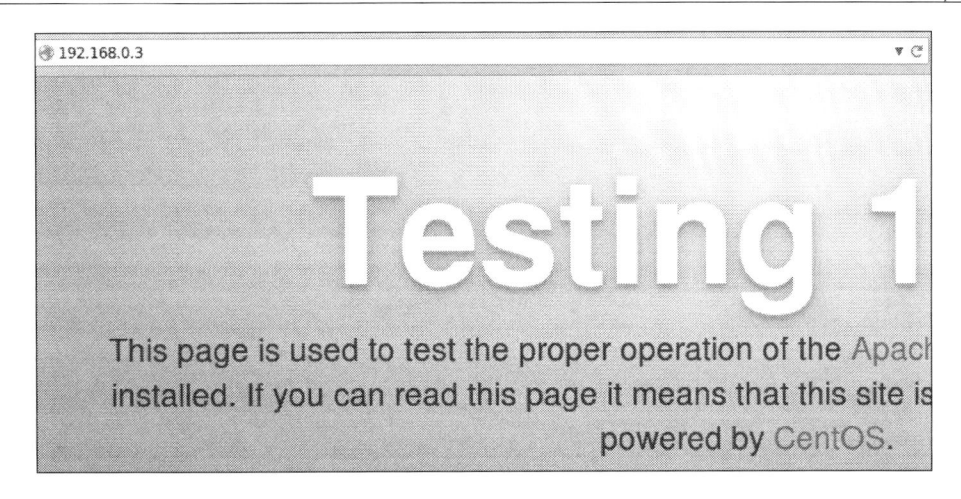

![Testing 123 page screenshot at 192.168.0.3 - "This page is used to test the proper operation of the Apache HTTP server after it has been installed. If you can read this page it means that this site is working properly. This server is powered by CentOS."]

Now, it is time to take a small step back. We will disable and stop Apache on both nodes so that the cluster will manage it when PCS is moving forward:

`systemctl disable httpd`

`systemctl stop httpd`

In order for Apache to listen on the virtual IP (to which we assigned `192.168.0.4` as the IP address) and the loopback address (we will see why in just a minute), we need to modify the main configuration file (`/etc/httpd/conf/httpd.conf`), as follows (you may want to make a backup of this file first):

```
# Listen: Allows you to bind Apache to specific IP addresses and/or
# ports, instead of the default. See also the <VirtualHost>
# directive.
#
# Change this to Listen on specific IP addresses as shown below to
# prevent Apache from glomming onto all bound IP addresses.
#
#Listen 12.34.56.78:80
Listen 192.168.0.4:80
Listen 127.0.0.1
```

Then, restart Apache:

`systemctl restart httpd`

Note that while restarting the web server in the second node, an error is to be expected since there is already a service running in that socket. However, that is normal, and now, you should be able to access the Apache welcome page by pointing your browser to the virtual IP.

The fun part is finding out which is the node in which the virtual IP was started, as shown in the following screenshot. If you get an error here instead, make sure `virtual_ip` is started by PCS first:

`pcs status | grep virtual_ip`

```
[root@node02 ~]# pcs status | grep virtual_ip
 virtual_ip     (ocf::heartbeat:IPaddr2):       Started node01
[root@node02 ~]#
```

Now, let's stop the cluster in that node, using the following command:

`pcs resource show virtual_ip`

Then, on the other node, it should still indicate that the resource is active.

However, even when the virtual IP is failed over to `node02`, the web server is not accessible through that resource because it wasn't started there in the first place. For this reason, we still need to configure Apache as a cluster resource so that it can be managed as such.

Configuring the web server as a cluster resource

You will recall from when we configured the virtual IP in *Chapter 2*, *Installing Cluster Services and Configuring Network Components*, and when we added replicated storage earlier during this chapter that we must indicate a way for PCS to check on a periodic basis whether the resource is available or not.

In this case, we will use the server status page (http://node0[1-2]/server-status), which is the preferred Apache web page as it provides information about how well the server will be performing PCS will query this page once per minute. This is accomplished by creating a file named status.conf inside /etc/httpd/conf.d on both nodes:

```
<Location /server-status>
  SetHandler server-status
  Order deny,allow
  Deny from all
  Allow from 127.0.0.1
</Location>
```

Then, with the following command, we will add Apache as a cluster resource. The status of the resource will be checked by PCS once every minute:

```
pcs resource create webserver ocf:heartbeat:apache configfile=/etc/httpd/conf/httpd.conf statusurl="http://localhost/server-status" op monitor interval=1min
```

By default, pacemaker will try to balance the resource usage over the cluster. However, at certain times, our setup will require that two related resources (as it is in the case of the web server and the virtual IP) need to run on the same host.

The web server should always run on the host on which the virtual IP is active. This also means that if the virtual IP resource is not active on any node, the web server should not run at all. In addition, since we need the web server to listen on the virtual IP address as well as on the loopback device on each host, it goes without saying that

We must ensure that the virtual IP resource is started before the web server resource.

We can accomplish both requirements through the use of the following constraints:

```
pcs constraint colocation add webserver with virtual_ip INFINITY
pcs constraint order virtual_ip then webserver
```

After running the second command, you should see the following message on your screen. Note that starting the virtual IP resource before the web server is a mandatory requirement:

```
Adding virtual_ip webserver (kind: Mandatory) (Options: first-action=start then-action=start)
```

Now, let's check the status of the cluster and focus on its assigned resources, as shown in the following screenshot:

```
[root@node01 ~]# pcs status
Cluster name: MyCluster
Last updated: Sat Apr 25 01:11:14 2015
Last change: Sat Apr 25 00:47:48 2015 via crm_attribute on node02
Stack: corosync
Current DC: node02 (2) - partition with quorum
Version: 1.1.12-a14efad
2 Nodes configured
4 Resources configured


Online: [ node01 node02 ]

Full list of resources:

 virtual_ip     (ocf::heartbeat:IPaddr2):       Started node01
 Master/Slave Set: web_drbd_clone [web_drbd]
     Masters: [ node02 ]
     Slaves: [ node01 ]
 webserver      (ocf::heartbeat:apache):        Started node01

PCSD Status:
  node01: Online
  node02: Online

Daemon Status:
  corosync: active/enabled
  pacemaker: active/enabled
  pcsd: active/enabled
[root@node01 ~]#
```

You can now simulate a failover by forcing `node01` to go offline. To do so, you can run the following command:

```
pcs cluster stop
```

The resources should be automatically started on `node02`, as indicated in the following screenshot:

```
[root@node02 ~]# pcs status
Cluster name: MyCluster
Last updated: Sat Apr 25 01:13:27 2015
Last change: Sat Apr 25 00:47:48 2015 via crm_attribute on node02
Stack: corosync
Current DC: node02 (2) - partition with quorum
Version: 1.1.12-a14efad
2 Nodes configured
4 Resources configured


Online: [ node02 ]
OFFLINE: [ node01 ]

Full list of resources:

 virtual_ip     (ocf::heartbeat:IPaddr2):       Started node02
 Master/Slave Set: web_drbd_clone [web_drbd]
     Masters: [ node02 ]
     Stopped: [ node01 ]
 webserver      (ocf::heartbeat:apache):        Started node02

PCSD Status:
  node01: Online
  node02: Online

Daemon Status:
  corosync: active/enabled
  pacemaker: active/enabled
  pcsd: active/enabled
[root@node02 ~]#
```

The last step consists of mounting the DRBD resource on the `/var/html/www` `directory` and adding in it a simple PHP page to display the PHP configuration of the cluster. You will then be able to build on that simple example to add more sophisticated applications.

Before attempting to use `/dev/drbd0`, we should check its status on both nodes with `drbd-overview`. If the output shows StandAlone or WFConnection, we are looking at a split-brain situation, which can be confirmed in the output of the following command:

`dmesg | grep -i brain`

This will result in a `Split-Brain detected, dropping connection!` error message.

Linbit recommends to manually resolve such cases by choosing a node whose modifications will be discarded and then issuing the following commands in it:

```
drbdadm secondary [resource name]
drbdadm connect --discard-my-data [resource name]
```

Then connect the DRBD resource on the other node:

```
drbdadm connect [resource name]
```

You can also start or stop DRBD and get an overview with the following commands in `node01`:

```
drbdadm up drbd0
drbdadm down drbd0
drbd-overview
ssh node02 drbdadm up drbd0
ssh node02 drbdadm down drbd0
ssh node02 drbd-overview
```

> Review the DRBD documentation carefully before choosing a recovery method after a split-brain situation. Since there is no one-size-fits-all answer to this issue, I have chosen to cover the recommended method in this book.

Mounting the DRBD resource and using it with Apache

Before using the DRBD resource, you must define a filesystem on it and mount it on a local directory. We will use Apache's document root directory (`/var/www/html`), but given the case, you could use a virtual host directory as well. As we did earlier, we will add these changes in a configuration file, step by step, and we will push it to the running CIB later on `node01` (or whatever the DC is).

To begin, create a new configuration file named `fs_dbrd0_cfg` (feel free to change the name if you want):

```
pcs cluster cib fs_drbd0_cfg
```

Next, we'll create the filesystem resource itself (again, change the variable values if needed). This is another special type of resource provided out of the box:

```
pcs -f fs_drbd0_cfg resource create web_fs Filesystem device="/dev/drbd0" directory="/var/www/html" fstype="ext4"
```

It indicates that the filesystem should always be available on the master DRBD resource:

```
pcs -f fs_drbd0_cfg constraint colocation add web_fs with web_drbd_clone INFINITY with-rsc-role=Master
```

Note that in order for the filesystem to be started properly, /dev/drbd0 must be started first, so we will have to add a constraint for this purpose:

```
pcs -f fs_drbd0_cfg constraint order promote web_drbd_clone then start web_fs
```

Finally, ensure that Apache needs to run on the same node as the filesystem resource, which also needs to come online before the web server resource can be started:

```
pcs -f fs_drbd0_cfg constraint colocation add webserver with web_fs INFINITY
pcs -f fs_drbd0_cfg constraint order web_fs then webserver
```

You can review the configuration with the following command:

```
pcs -f fs_drbd0_cfg constraint
```

The output is shown in the following screenshot:

```
[root@node01 ~]# pcs -f fs_drbd0_cfg constraint order web_fs then webserver
Adding web_fs webserver (kind: Mandatory) (Options: first-action=start then-action=start)
[root@node01 ~]# pcs -f fs_drbd0_cfg constraint
Location Constraints:
  Resource: virtual_ip
    Enabled on: node01 (score:INFINITY)
  Resource: webserver
    Enabled on: node01 (score:INFINITY)
Ordering Constraints:
  start virtual_ip then start webserver (kind:Mandatory)
  promote web_drbd_clone then start web_fs (kind:Mandatory)
  start web_fs then start webserver (kind:Mandatory)
Colocation Constraints:
  webserver with virtual_ip (score:INFINITY)
  web_fs with web_drbd_clone (score:INFINITY) (with-rsc-role:Master)
  webserver with web_fs (score:INFINITY)
[root@node01 ~]#
```

Real-world Implementations of Clustering

If everything is correct, then push it to the running CIB with this command:

```
pcs cluster cib-push fs_drbd0_cfg
```

The preceding command should show CIB updated on successful completion.

If you now run `pcs status`, you should see the newly added resources, as you can see in the following screenshot:

```
[root@node01 ~]# pcs status
Cluster name: MyCluster
Last updated: Mon Apr 27 15:17:43 2015
Last change: Mon Apr 27 15:17:36 2015 via crm_attribute on node02
Stack: corosync
Current DC: node02 (2) - partition with quorum
Version: 1.1.12-a14efad
2 Nodes configured
5 Resources configured


Online: [ node01 node02 ]

Full list of resources:

 virtual_ip     (ocf::heartbeat:IPaddr2):       Started node01
 Master/Slave Set: web_drbd_clone [web_drbd]
     Masters: [ node01 ]
     Slaves: [ node02 ]
 webserver      (ocf::heartbeat:apache):        Started node01
 web_fs (ocf::heartbeat:Filesystem):    Started node01

PCSD Status:
  node01: Online
  node02: Online

Daemon Status:
  corosync: active/enabled
  pacemaker: active/enabled
  pcsd: active/enabled
[root@node01 ~]#
```

Now, you don't need to manually mount /dev/drbd0 in /var/www/html, because the cluster will take care of it. You can verify that the DRBD device has been mounted in /var/www/html using this command:

`mount | grep drbd0`

> Remember that any original contents present in /var/html/www will not be available while /dev/drbd0 is mounted.

Testing the DRBD resource along with Apache

As a simple test, we will display the information about the PHP installation. Create a file named info.php inside /var/www/html on node01 with the following contents:

```
<?php
phpinfo();
?>
```

Now, point your browser to 192.168.0.4/info.php and verify that the output is similar to the one shown here:

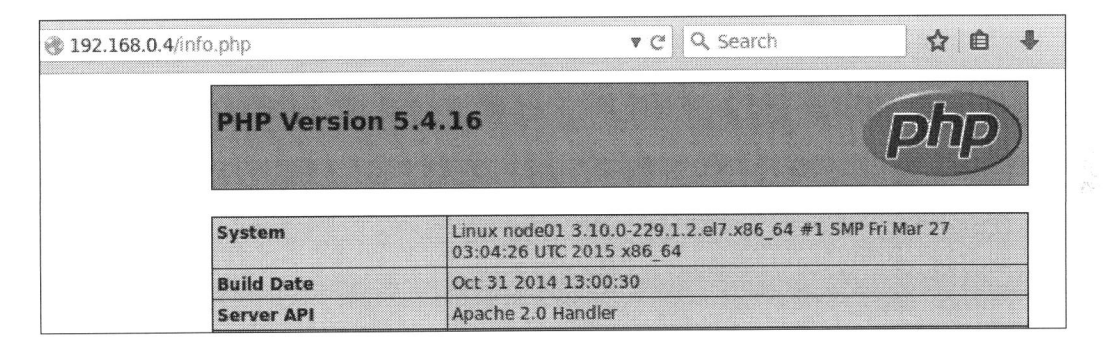

System	Linux node01 3.10.0-229.1.2.el7.x86_64 #1 SMP Fri Mar 27 03:04:26 UTC 2015 x86_64
Build Date	Oct 31 2014 13:00:30
Server API	Apache 2.0 Handler

PHP Version 5.4.16

Then, stop the cluster (`pcs cluster stop`) on node01 or put it into the standby mode (`pcs cluster standby node01`) and refresh the browser. The only thing that should change on the output is the system name, as shown in the following screenshot, since the `phinfo()` PHP function returns the local hostname along with the information about the PHP installation:

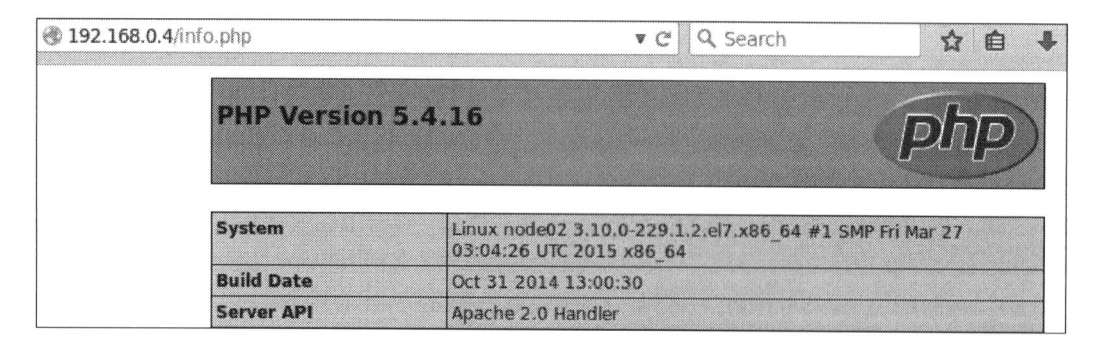

System	Linux node02 3.10.0-229.1.2.el7.x86_64 #1 SMP Fri Mar 27 03:04:26 UTC 2015 x86_64
Build Date	Oct 31 2014 13:00:30
Server API	Apache 2.0 Handler

In addition, if you list the contents of /var/www/html on node02, you will see that the info.php file that was created originally on node01 now shows on node02 as well, as indicated in this screenshot:

```
[root@node02 ~]# ls -l /var/www/html
total 20
-rw-r--r--. 1 root root    20 Apr 27 15:33 info.php
drwx------. 2 root root 16384 Apr 15 11:31 lost+found
[root@node02 ~]#
```

Before proceeding, remember to return node01 to normal mode:

`pcs cluster unstandby node01`

Setting up a high-availability database with replicated storage

The last part of this chapter focuses on setting up a HA MariaDB database with replicated storage. To begin, we will have to set up another DRBD resource as we did earlier. We will review the necessary steps here for clarity:

1. Add another virtual disk to each virtual machine (a 2 GB disk will do).

2. Create a partition on the newly added disk and then go through the process of creating a **Physical Volume** (PV) on /dev/sdc1, a **Volume Group** (VG, named drbd_db_vg), and finally a **Logical Volume** (LV, drbd_db_vol):

```
parted /dev/sdc mklabel msdos
parted /dev/sdc mkpart p 0% 100%
pvcreate /dev/sdc1
vgcreate drbd_db_vg /dev/sdc1
lvcreate -n drbd_db_vol -l 100%FREE drbd_db_vg
```

3. Create a configuration file (/etc/drbd.d/drbd1.res) for the new DRBD resource (drbd1), and based on the configuration file for the first replicated storage resource, edit the settings accordingly and use a different port:

```
resource drbd1 {
        disk /dev/drbd_db_vg/drbd_db_vol;
        device /dev/drbd1;
        meta-disk internal;
        on node01 {
                address 192.168.0.2:7790;
        }
        on node02 {
                address 192.168.0.3:7790;
        }
}
```

The, add a firewall rule to allow traffic:

```
iptables -I INPUT -p tcp -m state --state NEW -m tcp --dport 7790 -j ACCEPT
service iptables save
```

4. Repeat the previous steps on the second node. Initialize the metadata for the new DRBD resource on both nodes:

```
drbdadm create-md dbrd1
```

5. Enable the replicated storage resource in order to allocate disk and network resources for its operation:

```
drbdadm up drbd1
```

6. Mark the DRBD device on the DC node as primary:

```
drbdadm primary --force drbd1
```

Real-world Implementations of Clustering

7. Add the new DRBD device as cluster resource:

   ```
   mkdir -p /var/lib/mariadb_drbd1/data
   pcs cluster cib drbd1_conf
   pcs -f drbd1_conf resource create db_drbd ocf:linbit:drbd drbd_resource=drbd1 op monitor interval=60s
   pcs -f drbd1_conf resource master db_drbd_clone db_drbd master-max=1 master-node-max=1 clone-max=2 clone-node-max=1 notify=true
   pcs -f fs_drbd1_cfg resource create db_fs Filesystem device="/dev/drbd1" directory="/var/lib/mariadb_drbd1" fstype="ext4"
   pcs cluster cib-push drbd1_conf
   ```

When this process is complete, the overview of all configured DRBD resources up until this point should look like this:

```
[root@node01 ~]# cat /proc/drbd
version: 8.4.6 (api:1/proto:86-101)
GIT-hash: 833d830e0152d1e457fa7856e71e11248ccf3f70 build by phil@Build64R7, 2015-04-10 05:13:52
 0: cs:Connected ro:Primary/Secondary ds:UpToDate/UpToDate C r-----
    ns:98324 nr:0 dw:32888 dr:66457 al:11 bm:0 lo:0 pe:0 ua:0 ap:0 ep:1 wo:f oos:0
 1: cs:Connected ro:Primary/Secondary ds:UpToDate/UpToDate C r-----
    ns:2092956 nr:0 dw:33996 dr:2094412 al:0 bm:0 lo:0 pe:0 ua:0 ap:0 ep:1 wo:f oos:0
[root@node01 ~]# drbd-overview
 0:drbd0/0  Connected Primary/Secondary UpToDate/UpToDate /var/www/html ext4 2.0G 6.1M 1.9G 1%
 1:drbd1/0  Connected Primary/Secondary UpToDate/UpToDate
[root@node01 ~]#
```

In addition, the cluster should now include the new DRBD resource and its clone (`db_drbd` and `db_drbd_clone`, respectively) as well as the filesystem resource, as you can see in this screenshot:

```
Full list of resources:

virtual_ip      (ocf::heartbeat:IPaddr2):       Started node02
Master/Slave Set: web_drbd_clone [web_drbd]
    Masters: [ node02 ]
    Stopped: [ node01 ]
webserver       (ocf::heartbeat:apache):        Started node02
web_fs (ocf::heartbeat:Filesystem):     Started node02
Master/Slave Set: db_drbd_clone [db_drbd]
    Masters: [ node02 ]
    Stopped: [ node01 ]
db_fs  (ocf::heartbeat:Filesystem):    Started node02
dbserver        (ocf::heartbeat:mysql): Started node02
```

We can now divide the MariaDB files into two separate sections:

- Binaries, socket, and .pid files will be placed inside a directory on a regular partition, independent on each node (/var/lib/mysql by default). These are files we don't need to be highly available or fail-safe.
- Database and configuration files (my.cnf) will be stored in a DRBD resource, which will be mounted under /var/lib/mariadb_drbd1, inside a directory named data.

Next, we need to add the database server as a cluster resource:

```
pcs resource create dbserver ocf:heartbeat:mysql config="/var/lib/
mariadb_drbd1/my.cnf" datadir="/var/lib/mariadb_drbd1/data" op monitor
interval="30s" op start interval="0" timeout="60s" op stop interval="0"
timeout="60s"
```

This we will add the same constraints that we did with Apache:

```
pcs constraint colocation add dbserver with virtual_ip INFINITY

pcs constraint order virtual_ip then dbserver

pcs constraint colocation add db_drbd_clone with virtual_ip INFINITY

pcs constraint order virtual_ip then db_drbd_clone
```

Next, we will add a firewall rule to allow traffic:

```
iptables -I INPUT -p tcp -m state --state NEW -m tcp --dport 3306 -j
ACCEPT

service iptables save
```

We will begin by creating an `ext4` filesystem on `drbd1` and mounting it in the directory that was created previously. Only perform this step on the DC:

```
mkfs.ext4 /dev/drbd1
mount /dev/drbd1 /var/lib/mariadb_drbd1
```

Next, we need to move the database server configuration file to the mount point of `drbd1` (perform all of the following steps on both nodes):

```
mv /etc/my.cnf /var/lib/mariadb_drbd1/my.cnf
```

Edit it so that the `datadir` variable will point to the right directory inside the mount point of the DRBD resource and at the same time, specify that the database server should listen for TCP connections on a defined address (in this case, the IP address of our virtual IP resource):

```
datadir=/var/lib/mariadb_drbd1/data
bind-address=192.168.0.4
```

Next, we need to initialize the database data directory:

```
mysql_install_db --no-defaults --datadir=/var/lib/mariadb_drbd1/data
```

Finally, log on to the database server:

```
mysql -h 192.168.0.4 -u root -p
```

Then, grant all permissions to the root user identified by the defined password:

```
GRANT ALL ON *.* TO 'root'@'%' IDENTIFIED BY 'MyDBpassword';
FLUSH PRIVILEGES;
```

> This permission set is only for testing and should be modified with the necessary security parameters before moving the cluster to a production environment.

Alternatively, we can create an empty database:

```
CREATE DATABASE cluster_db;
```

Finally, make sure the `mysql` user can access the `/var/lib/mariadb_drbd1` directory:

```
chown -R mysql:mysql /var/lib/mariadb_drbd1/
```

If we now failover, from the active node to the passive one, the actual database files within `datadir` will be replicated by DRBD to the same directory on the other node.

Troubleshooting

As explained previously, the output of `pcs status` under `Failed actions` will show you whether there are problems with the cluster resources and provide information as to what you should do in order to fix them.

Here is an example:

- `exit-reason='Config /var/lib/mariadb_drbd1/my.cnf doesn't exist'`: Make sure the configuration file for MariaDB exists and is identical on both nodes.
- `exit-reason='Couldn't find device [/dev/drbd1]. Expected /dev/??? to exist'`: The DRBD device was not created correctly. Review the instructions and try to create it.

As you can see, the exit reason will give you valuable information to troubleshoot and fix the issues you may have. If, after verifying the conditions outlined in the error messages, you are still experiencing issues with a particular resource, it is useful to clean up the operation history of a resource and redetect its current state:

`pcs resource cleanup [resource name]`

From Kamran, a real world problem scenario, which happens when the reader follows (or gets lost following) instructions in this chapter:

```
[root@node01 ~]# pcs status
Cluster name: MyCluster
Last updated: Tue May 12 17:07:04 2015
Last change: Tue May 12 16:54:03 2015
Stack: corosync
Current DC: node01 (1) - partition with quorum
Version: 1.1.12-a14efad
2 nodes configured
9 resources configured


Online: [ node01 node02 ]


Full list of resources:

 virtual_ip    (ocf::heartbeat:IPaddr2):    Started node02
 Master/Slave Set: web_drbd_clone [web_drbd]
```

[85]

Real-world Implementations of Clustering

```
        Masters: [ node01 ]
        Slaves: [ node02 ]
 webserver    (ocf::heartbeat:apache):    Stopped
 web_fs    (ocf::heartbeat:Filesystem):    Started node01
 dbserver    (ocf::heartbeat:mysql):    Stopped
 Master/Slave Set: db_drbd_clone [db_drbd]
        Masters: [ node02 ]
        Stopped: [ node01 ]
 db_fs    (ocf::heartbeat:Filesystem):    Stopped


Failed actions:
    dbserver_start_0 on node01 'not installed' (5): call=36,
status=complete, exit-reason='Config /var/lib/mariadb_drbd1/my.cnf
doesn't exist', last-rc-change='Tue May 12 17:01:09 2015', queued=0ms,
exec=66ms

    db_fs_start_0 on node01 'not installed' (5): call=41,
status=complete, exit-reason='Couldn't find device [/dev/drbd1].
Expected /dev/??? to exist', last-rc-change='Tue May 12 17:01:09 2015',
queued=0ms, exec=38ms

    dbserver_start_0 on node02 'not installed' (5): call=41,
status=complete, exit-reason='Config /var/lib/mariadb_drbd1/my.cnf
doesn't exist', last-rc-change='Tue May 12 17:01:09 2015', queued=0ms,
exec=91ms

    db_fs_start_0 on node02 'not installed' (5): call=32,
status=complete, exit-reason='Couldn't find device [/dev/drbd1].
Expected /dev/??? to exist', last-rc-change='Tue May 12 17:01:08 2015',
queued=0ms, exec=39ms



PCSD Status:
  node01: Online
  node02: Online

Daemon Status:
  corosync: active/enabled
  pacemaker: active/enabled
  pcsd: active/enabled
[root@node01 ~]#
```

Summary

In this chapter, we explained how to set up real-world applications of clusters: a database server and a web server. Both applications build upon a replicated storage device in a setup that increases availability by providing failover storage for regular and database files.

In the next two chapters, we will build upon the concepts and resources that we introduced here, troubleshoot common issues in cluster-based web and database servers, and prevent common bottlenecks in order to ensure the high availability of applications.

5
Monitoring the Cluster Health

In *Chapter 2, Installing Cluster Services and Configuring Network Components*, we mentioned that becoming familiar with PCS and its myriad options would be helpful along the path that might lead us to the installation of a full operational high availability cluster. Although during the previous chapters we confirmed how true that statement was, here we will make further use of PCS to monitor the performance and availability of our cluster in order to identify and prevent possible bottlenecks and troubleshoot any issue that may arise.

Cluster services and performance

Although every system administrator must be well acquainted with the widely used Linux commands, such as `top` and `ps`, to quickly report a snapshot of running daemons and other processes in each node, you must also learn to rely on the new utilities provided by CentOS 7 to start our node monitoring, which we have introduced in previous chapters. But even more importantly, we will also use PCS-based commands to gain further insight into our cluster and its resources.

Monitoring the node status

As you can guess, perhaps the first thing that you always need to check is the status of each node—whether they are online or offline. Otherwise, there is little point in proceeding with further availability and performance analysis.

If you have a network management system (such as **Zabbix** or **Nagios**) server, you can easily monitor the status of your cluster members and receive alerts when they are unreachable. If not, you must come up with a supplementary solution of your own (which may not be as effective or errorproof) that you can use to detect when a node has gone offline.

Monitoring the Cluster Health

One such solution is a simple bash script (we will name it `pingreport.sh`, save it inside `/root/scripts`, and make it executable with `chmod +x /root/scripts/pingreport.sh`) which will periodically ping your nodes from another host and report via an e-mail to the system administrator if one of them is offline in order for you to take appropriate action. The following shell script does just that for nodes with IP addresses `192.168.0.2` and `192.168.0.3` (you can add as many nodes in the NODES variable, which will be used in the following for loop, but remember to separate them with a blank space). If both nodes are pingable, the report will be empty and no e-mails will be sent.

In order to take advantage of the following script, you will need to have an e-mail solution in place in order to send out alerts. In this case, we use the mail tool called mailx, which is available after installing a package (`yum install mailx`):

```bash
#!/bin/bash

# Directory where the ping script is located
DIR=/root/scripts

# Hostname or IP of remote host (to send alerts to)
REMOTEHOST="192.168.0.5"

# Name of report file
PING_REPORT="ping_report.txt"

# Make sure the current file is empty
cat /dev/null > $DIR/$PING_REPORT

#Current date to be used in the ping script
CURRENT_DATE=$(date +'%Y-%m-%d %H:%M')

# Node list
NODES="node01 node02"

# Loop through the list of nodes
for node in $NODES
    do
    LOST_PACKETS=$(ping -c 4 $node | grep -i unreachable | wc -l)
    if [ $LOST_PACKETS -ne "0" ]
```

```
                then
                        echo "$"LOST_PACKETS packets were missed while pinging $node
at $CURRENT_DATE" >> $DIR/$PING_REPORT
        fi
done


# Mail the report unless it's' empty
if [ -s "$"DIR/$PING_REPORT" ]
        then
        mail root@$REMOTEHOST -s "Ping report" -a $DIR/$PING_REPORT
fi
```

Even though the preceding script is enough to determine whether a node is pingable or not, you can tweak that script as you like, and then add it to cron in order for it to run automatically on the desired frequency. For example, the following cron job will execute the script every five minutes, regardless of the day:

`*/5 * * * * /root/scripts/pingreport.sh`

If you want to run the script manually, you can do so as follows:

`/root/scripts/pingreport.sh`

The following example indicates that both `192.168.0.2` and `192.168.0.3` were not pingable when the script was last run. Note that for simplicity, the script was executed from `node01`, a cluster member; however, under normal circumstances, you will want to use a separate host for this:

```
Message  1:
From root@node01.localdomain  Thu May 21 17:39:59 2015
Return-Path: <root@node01.localdomain>
X-Original-To: root@localhost
Delivered-To: root@localhost.localdomain
Date: Thu, 21 May 2015 17:39:59 -0400
To: root@localhost.localdomain
Subject: Ping report
User-Agent: Heirloom mailx 12.5 7/5/10
Content-Type: text/plain; charset=us-ascii
From: root@node01.localdomain (root)
Status: R

4 packets were missed while pinging 192.168.0.20 at 2015-05-21 17:39
4 packets were missed while pinging 192.168.0.30 at 2015-05-21 17:39
```

We will resume working with the script later in this chapter and extend its functionalities.

Now, it is time to dig a little deeper and view the status of the nodes configured in `corosync/pacemaker` with the following command:

`pcs status nodes pacemaker | corosync | both`

In the preceding command, a vertical bar is used to indicate mutually exclusive arguments.

In the following screenshot, you can see how `pcs status nodes both` returns the status of both `pacemaker` and `corosync` on both nodes:

```
[root@node02 ~]# pcs status nodes both
Corosync Nodes:
 Online: node01 node02
 Offline:
Pacemaker Nodes:
 Online: node01 node02
 Standby:
 Offline:
[root@node02 ~]#
```

> Although you can check the cluster's overall status with `pcs status`, as we have mentioned earlier, `pcs status nodes both` will give you the fine-grained node status information. You can stop one (or both) of the services on either node and run this same command to verify. This is equivalent to using `systemctl is-active pacemaker | corosync` on each node.

Monitoring the resources

As we have explained in the previous chapters, a cluster resource is a highly available service that is made available through at least one of the nodes. Among the resources that we configured up until this point, we can mention the virtual IP, the replicated storage device, the web server, and the database server. You can refer to *Chapter 4, Real-world Implementations of Clustering*, where we added constraints that indicated how (in what order) and where (in which node) the cluster resources should be started.

Either `pcs status` or `pcs resource show`, the preferred alternative, will list the names and status of all currently configured resources.

> If you specify a resource using its ID (that is, `pcs resource show virtual_ip`), you will see the options for the configured resource. On the other hand, if `--full` is specified (`pcs resource show --full`), all configured resource options will be displayed instead.

If a resource is started on the wrong node (for example, if it depends on a service that is currently active on another node), you will get an informative message when you attempt to use it. For example, the following screenshot shows that `dbserver` is started on `node02`, whereas its associated underlying storage device (`db_fs`) has been started on `node01`. You will recall from earlier chapters that this is part of the output of `pcs status`:

```
db_fs      (ocf::heartbeat:Filesystem):    Started node01
dbserver   (ocf::heartbeat:mysql):         Started node02
```

For this reason, if you attempt to log on to the database server using the virtual IP address (which is the common link to the cluster resources), you will get the error message indicated in the following screenshot telling you that you can't connect to the MariaDB instance:

```
[root@node01 ~]# mysql -u root -h 192.168.0.4 -p
Enter password:
ERROR 2003 (HY000): Can't connect to MySQL server on '192.168.0.4' (111)
[root@node01 ~]#
```

Let's see what happens (as shown in the next screenshot) when we move the `dbserver` resource to `node01` and enable it manually so that it starts right away. The following constraint is intended to cause `dbserver` to prefer `node01` so that it always runs on `node01` whenever such a node is available:

`pcs constraint location dbserver prefers node01=INFINITY`

`pcs resource restart dbserver`

```
db_fs      (ocf::heartbeat:Filesystem):    Started node01
dbserver   (ocf::heartbeat:mysql):         Started node01
```

Monitoring the Cluster Health

> If you need to remove a constraint, find out its id with `pcs constraint --full` and locate the associated resource. Then, delete it with `pcs constraint remove constraint_id`, where `constraint_id` is the identification as returned by the first command. You can also manually remove resources from one node to another with `pcs resource move <resource_id> <node_name>`, but be aware that the current constraints may or may not allow you to successfully complete the operation.

Now we can access the database server resource as expected, as shown here:

```
[root@node01 ~]# mysql -u root -h 192.168.0.4 -p
Enter password:
Welcome to the MariaDB monitor.  Commands end with ; or \g.
Your MariaDB connection id is 1
Server version: 5.5.41-MariaDB MariaDB Server

Copyright (c) 2000, 2014, Oracle, MariaDB Corporation Ab and others.

Type 'help;' or '\h' for help. Type '\c' to clear the current input statement.

MariaDB [(none)]> SHOW DATABASES;
+--------------------+
| Database           |
+--------------------+
| information_schema |
| cluster_db         |
| mysql              |
| performance_schema |
+--------------------+
4 rows in set (0.04 sec)

MariaDB [(none)]>
```

Once in a while, you may encounter some errors during or after a failover procedure or during boot—you name it. These messages are visible in the output of `pcs status`, as in the excerpt shown here:

```
Failed actions:
    dbserver_start_0 on node01 'not installed' (5): call=38, status=complete, exit-reason=
 21 19:16:30 2015', queued=0ms, exec=150ms
```

Before we proceed further, perhaps you will ask yourself: What if I want to save all available information about cluster problems to properly analyze and troubleshoot offline? If you are expecting PCS to have a tool to help you with that, you are right. Put a date and time following the `--from` and `--to` options and replace `dest` with a filename (a specific example is provided in the following command as well):

```
pcs cluster report [--from "YYYY-M-D H:M:S" [--to "YYYY-M-D" H:M:S"]]" dest
```

This will create a tarball containing every piece of information that is needed when reporting cluster problems. If `--from` and `--to` are not used, the report will include the data of the last 24 hours.

In the screenshot that will follow, we have omitted the `--from` and `--to` flags for brevity, and we can see yet another reason why setting up key-based authentication via `ssh` during *Chapter 1, Cluster Basics and Installation on CentOS 7* was not a mere suggestion—you have to report cluster information from both nodes.

In our case, we will execute the following command to obtain a tarball named `YYYY-MM-DD-report.tar.gz` in the current working directory. Note that the date part in the filename is for identification purposes only:

```
pcs cluster report $(date +%Y-%m-%d)-report
```

```
node02:     WARNING: The tarball produced by this program may contain
node02:             sensitive information such as passwords.
node02:
node02:
node02:
node02:     IT IS YOUR RESPONSIBILITY TO PROTECT SENSITIVE DATA FROM EXPOSURE
node02:
node02:     Calculated node list: node01 node02
node02:     Collecting data from node01 node02  (05/20/2015 07:50:00 PM to 05/21/2015 07:50:55 PM)
node01:     Including segment [1639-12554] from /var/log/messages
node01:     Including segment [189-8254] from /var/log/pacemaker.log
node01:     Including segment [1432165790-1432252265] from journald
node02:     Including segment [1963-10451] from /var/log/messages
node02:     Including segment [41-6215] from /var/log/pacemaker.log
node02:     Including segment [1432165790-1432252265] from journald
node02:
node02:     Collected results are available in /root/report.tar.gz.tar.gz
node02:
node02:     Please create a bug entry at
node02:         http://developerbugs.linux-foundation.org/enter_bug.cgi?product=Pacemaker
node02:     Include a description of your problem and attach this tarball
node02:
node02:     Thank you for taking time to create this report.
node02:
```

Monitoring the Cluster Health

Once the tarball with the report files has been created, you can untar and examine it. You will notice that it contains the files and directories seen in the following image. Before proceeding further, you may want to take a look at some of them, shown as follows:

```
tar xzf $(date +%Y-%m-%d)-report.tar.gz
cd $(date +%Y-%m-%d)-report
```

```
[root@node02 ~]# tar xzf $(date +%Y-%m-%d)-report.tar.gz
[root@node02 ~]# cd $(date +%Y-%m-%d)-report
[root@node02 2015-05-21-report]# ls
analysis.txt  collector  node01  node02  report.summary
```

Now, of course you want to purge records of the past failed actions that have been resolved. For this reason, PCS allows you to instruct the cluster to forget the operation history of a resource (or all of them), reset the fail count, and redetect the current states:

```
pcs resource cleanup <resource_id>
```

Note that if `resource_id` is not specified, then all resources/STONITH devices will be cleaned up.

Finally, while we are still talking about monitoring cluster resources, we might as well ask ourselves: Is there a way we can backup the current cluster configuration files and restore them later if needed, and can we easily go back to a previous configuration? The answer to both questions is yes—let's see how.

In order to back up the cluster configuration files, you will use the following command:

```
pcs config backup <filename>
```

Here, `<filename>` is a file identification of your choice to which PCS will append the `tar.bz2` extension after creating the tarball.

Consider the following example:

```
pcs config backup cluster_config_$(date +%Y-%m-%d)
```

This will result in the tarball backup with the contents shown in the following screenshot For our convenience, let us create a subdirectory named `cluster_config` inside our current working directory. We will use this newly created subdirectory to extract the contents of the report tarball:

```
mkdir cluster_config
```

```
tar xzf cluster_config_$(date +%Y-%m-%d).tar.bz2 -C cluster_config
ls -R cluster_config
```

```
[root@node01 ~]# ls | grep bz2
cluster_config.tar.bz2
[root@node01 ~]# tar xjf cluster_config.tar.bz2 --directory cluster_config
[root@node01 ~]# ls -R cluster_config
cluster_config:
cib.xml  corosync.conf  uidgid.d  version.txt

cluster_config/uidgid.d:
[root@node01 ~]#
```

> If you have followed the installation process step by step, as outlined in this book, bzip2 will most likely not be available. You will need to install it with `yum update && yum install bzip2` in order to untar the cluster configuration tarball.

Restoring the configuration is just as easy (you will need to stop the node and then start it again after the restoration process is completed), use the following command:

`pcs config restore [--local] <filename>`

This command will restore the backed-up cluster configuration files on all nodes using the backup as source. If you only need to restore the files on the current node, use the `--local` flag. Note that filename must be the `.tar.bz2` file (not the extracted files).

You can also go back to a certain point in time, as far as cluster configuration is concerned, using `pcs config checkpoint` with its associated options. With no options, `pcs config checkpoint` will list all available configuration checkpoints, as shown here:

```
[root@node01 ~]# pcs config checkpoint
checkpoint 32: date 2015-04-29 11:24:32
checkpoint 33: date 2015-04-29 11:24:32
checkpoint 34: date 2015-04-29 11:31:42
checkpoint 35: date 2015-04-29 11:31:46
checkpoint 36: date 2015-04-29 11:31:46
checkpoint 37: date 2015-04-29 11:38:16
checkpoint 38: date 2015-04-29 11:38:19
checkpoint 39: date 2015-04-29 11:38:19
checkpoint 40: date 2015-04-29 11:53:39
checkpoint 41: date 2015-04-29 11:53:42
checkpoint 42: date 2015-04-29 11:53:42
checkpoint 43: date 2015-04-29 11:54:00
checkpoint 44: date 2015-04-29 11:55:39
```

The `pcs config checkpoint view <checkpoint_number>` command displays to standard output the specified configuration checkpoint details, as shown in the next screenshot. Consider the following example:

`pcs config checkpoint view 1`

```
[root@node01 ~]# pcs config checkpoint view 1
Resources:
 Resource: virtual_ip (class=ocf provider=heartbeat type=IPaddr2)
  Attributes: ip=192.168.0.4 cidr_netmask=24 nic=enp0s3
  Operations: start interval=0s timeout=20s (virtual_ip-start-timeout-20s)
              stop interval=0s timeout=20s (virtual_ip-stop-timeout-20s)
              monitor interval=30s (virtual_ip-monitor-interval-30s)
 Master: web_drbd_clone
  Meta Attrs: master-max=1 master-node-max=1 clone-max=2 clone-node-max=1 notify=true
  Resource: web_drbd (class=ocf provider=linbit type=drbd)
   Attributes: drbd_resource=drbd0
   Operations: start interval=0s timeout=240 (web_drbd-start-timeout-240)
               promote interval=0s timeout=90 (web_drbd-promote-timeout-90)
               demote interval=0s timeout=90 (web_drbd-demote-timeout-90)
               stop interval=0s timeout=100 (web_drbd-stop-timeout-100)
```

The `pcs config checkpoint restore <checkpoint_number>` command restores cluster configuration to a specified checkpoint, which is why it's a great idea to check the details of the desired checkpoint before restoring.

When a resource refuses to start

Under normal circumstances, cluster resources will be managed automatically without much intervention from the system administrator. However, there will be times when something may prevent a resource from starting properly, and it will be necessary to take immediate action.

As the man page for PCS states,

> *Starting resources on a cluster is (almost) always done by pacemaker and not directly from PCS. If your resource isn't starting, it's usually due to either a misconfiguration of the resource (which you debug in the system log), or constraints preventing the resource from starting or the resource being disabled. You can use* `pcs resource debug-start` *to test resource configuration, but it should not normally be used to start resources in a cluster.*

Having said that, when `pacemaker` cannot, for some reason, properly start a resource, execute the following command:

`pcs resource debug-start <resource id> [--full]`

This will force the specified resource to start on the current node, ignoring the cluster recommendations. The result will be printed to the screen (use the `--full` flag to obtain more detailed output) and will provide helpful information to assist you in troubleshooting the resource and the cluster operation.

In the following screenshot, the output of `pcs resource debug-start virtual_ip --full` is truncated for the sake of brevity:

```
[root@node01 ~]# pcs resource debug-start virtual_ip --full
Operation start for virtual_ip (ocf:heartbeat:IPaddr2) returned 0
 >  stderr: + 12:50:42: 69: . /usr/lib/ocf/lib/heartbeat/findif.sh
 >  stderr: + 12:50:42: 72: OCF_RESKEY_lvs_support_default=false
 >  stderr: + 12:50:42: 73: OCF_RESKEY_lvs_ipv6_addrlabel_default=false
 >  stderr: + 12:50:42: 74: OCF_RESKEY_lvs_ipv6_addrlabel_value_default=99
 >  stderr: + 12:50:42: 75: OCF_RESKEY_clusterip_hash_default=sourceip-sourceport
 >  stderr: + 12:50:42: 76: OCF_RESKEY_unique_clone_address_default=false
 >  stderr: + 12:50:42: 77: OCF_RESKEY_arp_interval_default=200
 >  stderr: + 12:50:42: 78: OCF_RESKEY_arp_count_default=5
 >  stderr: + 12:50:42: 79: OCF_RESKEY_arp_bg_default=true
 >  stderr: + 12:50:42: 80: OCF_RESKEY_arp_mac_default=ffffffffffff
 >  stderr: + 12:50:42: 82: : false
 >  stderr: + 12:50:42: 83: : false
 >  stderr: + 12:50:42: 84: : 99
 >  stderr: + 12:50:42: 85: : sourceip-sourceport
 >  stderr: + 12:50:42: 86: : false
 >  stderr: + 12:50:42: 87: : 200
 >  stderr: + 12:50:42: 88: : 5
 >  stderr: + 12:50:42: 89: : true
 >  stderr: + 12:50:42: 90: : ffffffffffff
 >  stderr: + 12:50:42: 93: SENDARP=/usr/libexec/heartbeat/send_arp
 >  stderr: + 12:50:42: 94: SENDUA=/usr/libexec/heartbeat/send_ua
```

From this example, you can begin to glimpse how useful this command can be as it provides you with very detailed information, step by step, of the resource operation. For example, if the `dbserver` resource refuses to start and returns errors even after repeatedly having cleaned it up, run the following command:

`pcs resource debug-start dbserver --full | less`

With this, you will be able to view—with great detail—the steps that are usually performed by the cluster when trying to bring up such a resource. If this process fails at some point, you will be provided with a description of what went wrong and when, and then you will be better able to fix it.

Checking the availability of core components

Before wrapping up, let's go back to the first example (checking the online status of each node) and extend it so that we can also monitor the core components of the cluster framework, that is, `pacemaker`, `corosync`, and `pcsd`, as outlined earlier in *Chapter 2, Installing Cluster Services and Configuring Network Components*.

> In order to ensure a successful connection via `ssh` from a node to itself, you will need to copy its key to `authorized_keys` Thus, to enable passwordless user login for user root, run the following command on both nodes:
> `cp /root/.ssh/id_rsa.pub /root/.ssh/authorized_keys`

In the best case scenario, during a graceful failover, you will want to be notified whenever one (or more) of those services is stopped. Adding a few lines to the script will also check for the status of the corresponding daemons and alert you if they're down:

```bash
#!/bin/bash

# Directory where the ping script is located
DIR=/root/scripts

# Hostname or IP of remote host (to send alerts to)
REMOTEHOST="192.168.0.5"
# Name of report file
PING_REPORT="ping_report.txt"

# Make sure the current file is empty
cat /dev/null > $DIR/$PING_REPORT

#Current date to be used in the ping script
CURRENT_DATE=$(date +'%Y-%m-%d %H:%M')
# Node list
NODES="node01 node02"

# Outer loop: check each node
for node in $NODES
    do
    LOST_PACKETS=$(ping -c 4 $node | grep -i unreachable | wc -l)
    if [ $LOST_PACKETS -ne "0" ]
        then
```

```
                echo "$"LOST_PACKETS packets were missed while pinging
$node at $CURRENT_DATE" >> $DIR/$PING_REPORT
        fi
# Inner loop: check all cluster core components in each node
        for service in corosync pacemaker pcsd
        do
        IS_ACTIVE=$(ssh -qn $node systemctl is-active $service)
        if [ $IS_ACTIVE != "active" ]
                then
                echo "$"service is NOT active on $node. Please check
ASAP." >> $DIR/$PING_REPORT
        fi
        done
done

# Mail the report unless it's' empty
if [ -s "$"DIR/$PING_REPORT" ]
        then
        mail -s "Ping report" root@localhost < $DIR/$PING_REPORT
fi
```

As a simple test, stop the cluster (pcs cluster stop) on node02 (192.168.0.3), run the script from the monitoring host or from any node, and check your mail inbox to verify that it is working correctly. In the following screenshot, you can see an example of what it should look like:

```
From root@node01.localdomain  Fri May 22 13:59:16 2015
Return-Path: <root@node01.localdomain>
X-Original-To: root@localhost
Delivered-To: root@localhost.localdomain
Date: Fri, 22 May 2015 13:59:16 -0400
To: root@localhost.localdomain
Subject: Ping report
User-Agent: Heirloom mailx 12.5 7/5/10
Content-Type: text/plain; charset=us-ascii
From: root@node01.localdomain (root)
Status: RO

corosync is NOT active on 192.168.0.3. Please check ASAP.
pacemaker is NOT active on 192.168.0.3. Please check ASAP.
```

Summary

In this chapter, we have explained how to monitor, troubleshoot, and fix common cluster problems and needs. Not all of these will be undesired or unexpected as a sudden system crash. There will be times when you need to bring down the cluster and the resources it is running for some planned maintenance or during a power outage before your **uninterruptible power supply** (**UPS**) runs out.

Because prevention is your best ally in these circumstances, ensure that you routinely monitor the health of your cluster. Follow the procedures outlined in this chapter so that you don't run into any surprises when real emergencies come up. Specifically, under either real or simulated cases, ensure that you back up the cluster configuration, stop the cluster on both nodes separately, and then and only then, halt the node.

Measuring and Increasing Performance

Up to this point, we have created an active/passive cluster, added several resources to it, and tested its failover capabilities. We also discussed how to troubleshoot common issues. The final step in our journey consists of measuring and increasing the performance of our cluster as it has been installed so far—as far as the services running on it are concerned.

In addition, we will provide the overall instructions to convert your A/P cluster into an A/A one.

Setting up a sample database

In order to properly test our MariaDB database server, we need a database populated with sample data. For this reason, we will use the Employees database, developed by Patrick Crews and Giuseppe Maxia and provided by Oracle Corporation under a Creative Commons Attribution-Share Alike 3.0 Unported License. It provides a very large dataset (~160 MB and ~4 million records) spread over six tables, which will be ideal for our performance tests.

Measuring and Increasing Performance

> The Creative Commons Attribution-Share Alike 3.0 Unported License, available at http://creativecommons.org/licenses/by-sa/3.0/, grants us the following freedoms regarding the Employees database:
>
> *Share: This lets us copy and redistribute the material in any medium or format*
>
> *Adapt: This lets us remix, transform, and build upon the material for any purpose, even commercially.*
>
> *The licensor cannot revoke these freedoms as long as you follow the license terms.*

Downloading and installing the Employees database

Let's proceed with downloading and installing the database using the following steps:

1. To download the Employees table, go to https://launchpad.net/test-db/ and grab the link for the tarball of the latest stable release (at the time of writing this book, it is v1.0.6), as shown in the following screenshot:

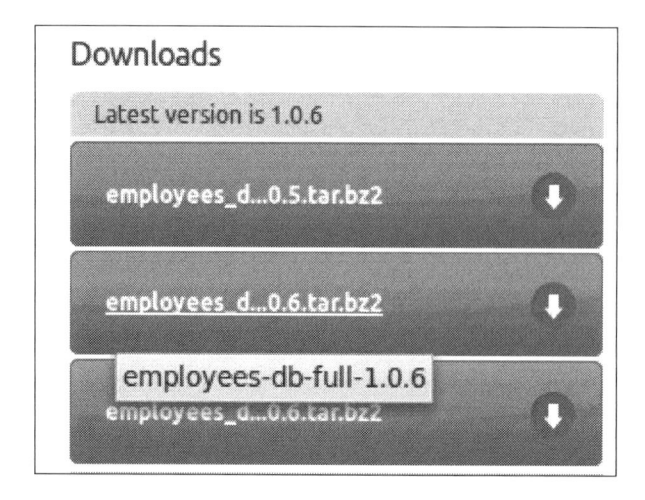

   Downloads
   Latest version is 1.0.6
   employees_d...0.5.tar.bz2
   employees_d...0.6.tar.bz2
   employees-db-full-1.0.6
   employees_d...0.6.tar.bz2

2. Then, download it to the node on which the database server is running (in our case, it is node01). To do so, you will need to install two packages named wget and bzip2 first, using the following command:

   ```
   yum -y install wget bzip2 && wget https://launchpad.net/test-db/employees-db-1/1.0.6/+download/employees_db-full-1.0.6.tar.bz2
   ```

Then, extract/unarchive its contents in your current working directory:

```
tar xjf employees_db-full-1.0.6.tar.bz2
```

3. This will create a subdirectory named `employees_db`, where the main installation script (`employees.sql`) resides, as can be seen in the output of the following two commands:

```
cd employees_db
ls
```

4. Next, use the following command to connect to the cluster database server we set up and configured in *Chapter 4, Real-world Implementations of Clustering* (note that you will be prompted to enter the password for the root MariaDB user):

```
mysql -h 192.168.0.4 -u root -p -t < employees.sql
```

5. This will also install the employees database and load the corresponding information into its tables:

- `departments`
- `employees`
- `dept_emp`
- `dept_manager`
- `titles`
- `salaries`

> After you are done setting up the sample database, feel free to perform a forced failover to verify that the resources and the database, along with their tables and records, become available in the current passive node. Review chapter 4 to recall instructions if you need.

Due to the high volume of data being loaded into the database, it is to be expected that the installation may take around a minute or two to complete. While we are at it, we will see the progress of the import process: the database structure and the storage engine are instantiated, then the tables are created, and finally, they are populated with data, as shown here:

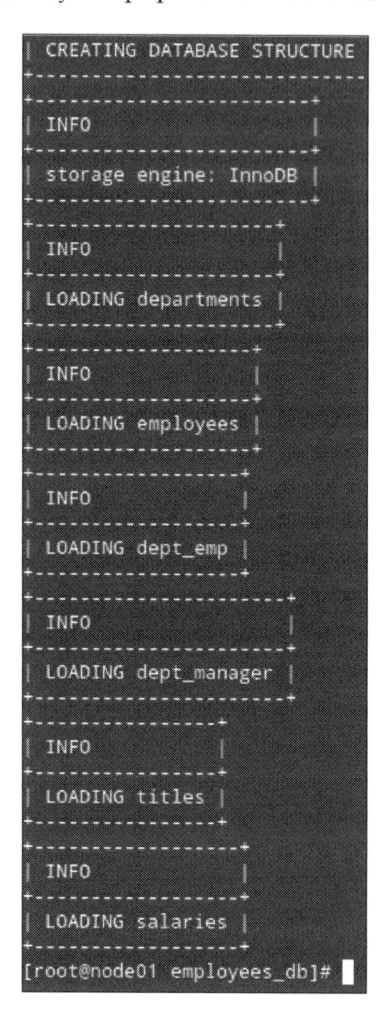

```
| CREATING DATABASE STRUCTURE |
+-----------------------------+
| INFO                        |
+-----------------------------+
| storage engine: InnoDB      |
+-----------------------------+

+-----------------------------+
| INFO                        |
+-----------------------------+
| LOADING departments         |
+-----------------------------+

+-----------------------------+
| INFO                        |
+-----------------------------+
| LOADING employees           |
+-----------------------------+

+-----------------------------+
| INFO                        |
+-----------------------------+
| LOADING dept_emp            |
+-----------------------------+

+-----------------------------+
| INFO                        |
+-----------------------------+
| LOADING dept_manager        |
+-----------------------------+

+-----------------------------+
| INFO                        |
+-----------------------------+
| LOADING titles              |
+-----------------------------+

+-----------------------------+
| INFO                        |
+-----------------------------+
| LOADING salaries            |
+-----------------------------+
[root@node01 employees_db]#
```

6. We can verify by logging into the database server and issuing these commands to first list all databases. Then, switch to the recently installed Employees database, and use it for the subsequent queries:

   SHOW DATABASES;

   USE employees;

   SHOW TABLES;

7. The output should be similar to the one shown in the preceding screenshot.

```
MariaDB [(none)]> SHOW DATABASES;
+--------------------+
| Database           |
+--------------------+
| information_schema |
| employees          |
| mysql              |
| performance_schema |
+--------------------+
4 rows in set (0.00 sec)

MariaDB [(none)]> USE employees;
Reading table information for completion of table and column names
You can turn off this feature to get a quicker startup with -A

Database changed
MariaDB [employees]> SHOW TABLES;
+---------------------+
| Tables_in_employees |
+---------------------+
| departments         |
| dept_emp            |
| dept_manager        |
| employees           |
| salaries            |
| titles              |
+---------------------+
6 rows in set (0.00 sec)

MariaDB [employees]>
```

8. Before we proceed with the actual performance tests (measuring general performance before and after a failover event), feel free to investigate those tables (and the fields they contain) using the DESCRIBE statement. Then browse the records with the SELECT statement, as shown here:

```
DESCRIBE salaries;
SELECT * FROM salaries LIMIT 5;
```

9. The result can be seen in the following screenshot:

```
MariaDB [employees]> DESCRIBE salaries;
+-----------+---------+------+-----+---------+-------+
| Field     | Type    | Null | Key | Default | Extra |
+-----------+---------+------+-----+---------+-------+
| emp_no    | int(11) | NO   | PRI | NULL    |       |
| salary    | int(11) | NO   |     | NULL    |       |
| from_date | date    | NO   | PRI | NULL    |       |
| to_date   | date    | NO   |     | NULL    |       |
+-----------+---------+------+-----+---------+-------+
4 rows in set (0.00 sec)

MariaDB [employees]> SELECT * FROM salaries LIMIT 5;
+--------+--------+------------+------------+
| emp_no | salary | from_date  | to_date    |
+--------+--------+------------+------------+
|  10001 |  60117 | 1986-06-26 | 1987-06-26 |
|  10001 |  62102 | 1987-06-26 | 1988-06-25 |
|  10001 |  66074 | 1988-06-25 | 1989-06-25 |
|  10001 |  66596 | 1989-06-25 | 1990-06-25 |
|  10001 |  66961 | 1990-06-25 | 1991-06-25 |
+--------+--------+------------+------------+
5 rows in set (0.01 sec)
```

Once you have taken some time to become acquainted with the structure of the database, we are ready to proceed with the tests.

Introducing initial cluster tests

In addition, for the actual performance tests, you should note that MariaDB comes with several database-related utilities that can come in handy for a variety of administration tasks. One of them is `mysqlshow`, which returns complete information about databases and tables in one quick command.

Its generic syntax is as follows:

```
mysqlshow [options] [db_name [tbl_name [col_name]]]
```

So, we could use the following command to display the description for the titles table in the `employees` database:

```
mysqlshow employees titles -h 192.168.0.4 -u root -p
```

> You can list the complete set of utilities that are included in your MariaDB installation using the `ls /bin | grep mysql` command. Each of those tools has a corresponding manual page, which can be invoked from the command line as usual.

We will use another of the tools that are included by MariaDB to see how our database server performs when placed under significant load. The tool is `mysqlslap`, a diagnostic program designed to emulate client load for a MariaDB/MySQL server and to report the timing of each stage. It works as if multiple clients are accessing the server simultaneously.

Before executing the actual commands that we will use in the following tests, we will introduce a few of the flags available for `mysqlslap`:

- `--create-schema`: This command specifies the database in which we will run the tests
- `--query`: This is a string (or alternatively, a file) containing the SELECT statements used to retrieve data
- `--delimiter`: This command allows you to specify a delimiter to separate multiple queries in the same string in `--query`
- `--concurrency`: This command is the number of simultaneous connections to simulate
- `--iterations`: This is the number of times to run the tests
- `--number-of-queries`: This command limits each client (refer to `--concurrency`) to that amount of queries

In addition, there are other switches listed in the manual page for `mysqlslap` that you can use if you want.

That said, we will run the following tests against the database server in our cluster.

Test 1 – retrieving all fields from all records

In this first test, we will perform a rather simple query that consists of retrieving all fields from all records in the employees table. We will simulate 10 concurrent connections and make 50 queries overall. This will result in clients running 5 queries each (50/10 = 5):

```
mysqlslap --create-schema=employees --query="SELECT * FROM employees"
--concurrency=10 --iterations=2 --number-of-queries=50 -h 192.168.0.4 -u
root -p
```

After a couple of minutes, you will be able to see output similar to the one shown in the following screenshot. Although here we list the result of an isolated test, you may want to perform this operation several times on your own and write down the results for a later comparison. However, if you choose to do so, make sure that the query results are not cached by running the following command in your MariaDB server session after each run:

```
RESET QUERY CACHE;
```

```
Benchmark
        Average number of seconds to run all queries: 20.770 seconds
        Minimum number of seconds to run all queries: 20.242 seconds
        Maximum number of seconds to run all queries: 21.298 seconds
        Number of clients running queries: 10
        Average number of queries per client: 5
```

Test 2 – performing JOIN operations

In this second test, we will do a `JOIN` operation between the employees and salaries tables (a more realistic example) and modify the number of connections, queries, and iterations a bit:

```
mysqlslap --create-schema=employees --query="SELECT A.first_name, A.last_name, B.salary FROM employees A JOIN salaries B on A.emp_no = B.emp_no" --concurrency=3 --number-of-queries=12 --iterations=2 -h 192.168.0.4 -u root -p
```

In the following screenshot, we can see an expected increase in the time it took to run the queries this time:

```
Benchmark
        Average number of seconds to run all queries: 40.008 seconds
        Minimum number of seconds to run all queries: 38.713 seconds
        Maximum number of seconds to run all queries: 41.304 seconds
        Number of clients running queries: 3
        Average number of queries per client: 4
```

Before proceeding further, feel free to play around with the number of connections, iterations, and queries, or with the query itself. Based on these values, you may knock the database server down. That is to be expected at some point, since we have been building our infrastructure and examples on a virtual machine-based cluster. For this reason, you may want to increase the processing resources on each node's Virtualbox configuration to the extent of the available capacity, or consider acquiring real hardware to set up your cluster.

> Database administration and optimization are topics out of the scope of this book. It is strongly recommended that you also take these subjects into account before moving the cluster to a production environment. Since the performance of the database and web servers can be optimized separately through their corresponding settings, in this book, we will focus our efforts on analyzing and improving the availability of these resources (which we have named `dbserver` and `webserver` respectively) using their respective configuration files and internal settings.

Performing a failover

We will now force a failover by stopping the cluster functionality on the node where all the resources are currently running (`node01`) so that they will move to `node02`. Here, we will perform tests 1 and 2, and we expect to see a similar behavior to what we saw earlier. It is important to keep in mind that during a failover, data is not encrypted automatically. If you have concerns about sensitive data being failed over an unsecured connection, you should take the necessary precaution to use encryption either at the filesystem or at the Logical Volume level. Before we do this, however, we must keep in mind that moving a sensitive resource, such as a database server, around a cluster constantly may negatively impact the availability of such resource. For this reason, we will want it to remain in the node where it is active unless in the case that there is an actual node shutdown. The concept of resource stickiness does exactly this: it allows us to instruct all cluster resources to either fall back to their original node when it becomes available again after an outage, or to remain where they are currently active. The following syntax is used to specify the default value for all resources:

```
pcs resource defaults resource-stickiness=value
```

The higher the value, the more the resource will prefer to stay where it is. By default, Pacemaker uses 0 as value, which tells the cluster that it is desired (and optimal) to move the resource around in the case of failover. To specify the stickiness of a specific resource, use the following syntax to set the stickiness for a specific resource:

```
pcs resource meta <resource_id> stickiness=value
```

Let's assume that you use `INFINITY` as the value in the preceding command:

```
pcs resource defaults resource-stickiness=INFINITY
pcs resource meta <resource_id> stickiness=INFINITY
```

(Where you need to replace `resource_id` with the actual resource identification)

Measuring and Increasing Performance

Then, both the default stickiness for all resources and for the resource identified by `resource_id` will be set to `INFINITY`. That being said, let's now perform the failover. Take note of the current node and resource status by using the following command:

```
pcs status
```

Then, stop the cluster by using the following command:

```
pcs cluster stop
```

Then, verify that all resources have been properly started on the other node. If not, troubleshoot using the tools explained in *Chapter 5, Monitoring the Cluster Health*. Finally, proceed to run tests 1 and 2 on `node02`.

The results in our present case are explained here.

For test 1, refer to the following screenshot:

```
Benchmark
        Average number of seconds to run all queries: 20.179 seconds
        Minimum number of seconds to run all queries: 19.930 seconds
        Maximum number of seconds to run all queries: 20.428 seconds
        Number of clients running queries: 10
        Average number of queries per client: 5
```

For our convenience, let's put both results in the following for a quick comparison:

TEST 1 [seconds]	Node01	Node02
Average, all queries	20.770	20.179
Minimum, all queries	20.242	19.930
Maximum, all queries	21.298	20.428

Summarizing results of test 1 on both nodes

On the other hand, for test 2, the following screenshot and the next table show the details:

```
Benchmark
        Average number of seconds to run all queries: 39.084 seconds
        Minimum number of seconds to run all queries: 38.779 seconds
        Maximum number of seconds to run all queries: 39.389 seconds
        Number of clients running queries: 3
        Average number of queries per client: 4
```

TEST 2 [seconds]	Node01	Node02
Average, all queries	40.008	39.084
Minimum, all queries	38.713	38.779
Maximum, all queries	41.304	39.389

Summarizing results of test 2 on both nodes

As you can see, the results are very similar in both cases, which confirms that the failover did not affect the performance of the database server running on top of our cluster. While it is true that the failover did not improve performance either, we can see that the availability of the resource during a failover has been confirmed with a negative impact on the functionality of the cluster.

Measuring and improving performance

You will recall from earlier chapters that by definition, a resource is a service that is made highly available by the cluster. Every resource is assigned what is called a **resource agent**, an external shell script that manages the actual resource for the cluster, independently of how those services would be managed by systemd if they were left to its care. Thus, the actual operation of the resource is transparent to the cluster, since it is being managed by the resource agent.

Resource agents are found inside `/usr/lib/ocf/resource.d`, so feel free to take a look at them to become better acquainted with their structure. In most circumstances, you will not need to modify them, but work on the specific resources' configuration files, as we shall see. You will recall from earlier chapters that adding a cluster resource involved using an argument of the `standard:provider:resource_agent` form (`ocf:heartbeat:mysql`, for example).You can also view the complete list of resource standards and providers with `pcs resource standards` and `pcs resource providers` respectively. Additionally, you can view the available agents for each `standard:provider` pair with `pcs resource agents standard:provider`.

Apache's configuration and settings

When the Apache web server is first installed, by default, it comes with several modules in the form of **Dynamic Shared Objects** (**DSOs**) that extend its functionality. The downside is that some of them may consume resources unnecessarily if they remain loaded and your applications don't' use them. As you can probably guess, this may lead to performance loss over time.

In CentOS 7, you can view the list of currently loaded and shared modules with `httpd -M`. The following output is truncated for the sake of brevity, but should be very similar in your case:

```
Loaded Modules:
 core_module (static)
 so_module (static)
 http_module (static)
 access_compat_module (shared)
 actions_module (shared)
 alias_module (shared)
 allowmethods_module (shared)
 auth_basic_module (shared)
 auth_digest_module (shared)
 authn_anon_module (shared)
 authn_core_module (shared)
```

A careful inspection of the module list and solid knowledge of what your applications actually needs will help you define which modules are not needed, and thus, they can be unloaded for the time being.

Look at the following line in `/etc/httpd/conf/httpd.conf`:

```
IncludeOptional conf.modules.d/*.conf
```

This line indicates that Apache will look in the `conf.modules.d` directory for instructions to load module inside `.conf` files. For example, in the standard installation, `00-base.conf` contains ~70 `LoadModule` directives that point to DSOs inside `/etc/httpd/modules`. It is in these `.conf` files that you can enable or disable (by prepending each `LoadModule` directive with a `#` symbol, thus commenting that line) Apache modules. Note that this must be performed on both nodes.

Loading and disabling modules

In the following screenshot, `userdir_module` modules, `version_module`, and `vhost_alias_module` are loaded, whereas `buffer_module`, `watchdog_module`, and `heartbeat_module` are disabled through `00-base.conf`:

```
LoadModule userdir_module modules/mod_userdir.so
LoadModule version_module modules/mod_version.so
LoadModule vhost_alias_module modules/mod_vhost_alias.so

#LoadModule buffer_module modules/mod_buffer.so
#LoadModule watchdog_module modules/mod_watchdog.so
#LoadModule heartbeat_module modules/mod_heartbeat.so
```

For example, in order to disable the `userdir` module, comment the corresponding `LoadModule` directive in `/etc/httpd/conf.modules.d/00-base.conf` on both nodes:

```
#LoadModule userdir_module modules/mod_userdir.so
```

Restart the cluster resource on the node where it is currently active:

`pcs resource restart webserver`

Placing limits on the number of Apache processes and children

In order for Apache to be able to handle as many simultaneous requests as needed, but preventing it from consuming more RAM than you can afford for your application(s), you need to set the `MaxRequestWorkers` (called `MaxClients` before version 2.3.13) directive to an appropriate value based mostly on the available physical memory that can be allotted in your specific environment. Note that if this value is set too high, you may bring the web server (and the resource altogether) to its knees.

On the other hand, setting it to an appropriate value, which is calculated based on the memory usage of each Apache process compared to the allotted RAM, will allow the web server to respond to that many requests at once. If the number of requests surpasses the capacity of the server, the extra requests will be served once the first ones have already been served, thus avoiding the resource from hanging for all connections.

For further details, refer to the Apache MPM Common directives documentation at `http://httpd.apache.org/docs/2.4/mod/mpm_common.html`. Keep in mind that Apache fine-tuning is out of the scope of this book, and the actions mentioned here are generally not enough for production use.

Database resource

Since you will seldom use a web server without an accompanying database server, you also need to look on that side of things to improve performance. Here are some basic things you will want to look at.

Creating indexes

A database containing tables of hundreds of thousands or million of records can quickly become a performance bottleneck when a typical `SELECT-FROM-WHERE` statement is made to retrieve a specific record. Going through every row in a table to accomplish this is considered highly inefficient as it is performed at the hard disk level.

With indexes, the operation is performed in memory instead of disk, and records can be automatically sorted so that it's faster to find the one we want because an index only contains the actual sorted data and a link to the original data record. In addition, we can create an index for each column we need to sort by, so using indexes becomes a handy tool to improve performance.

To begin, exit your MariaDB session and run test 3 to measure performance without indexes:

```
mysqlslap --create-schema=employees --query="SELECT * FROM employees WHERE emp_no=1007" --concurrency=15 --number-of-queries=150 --iterations=10 -h 192.168.0.4 -u root -p
```

Now, let's create indexes on the `emp_no` field in the employees and salaries tables since we will use them in our `WHERE` clause, and then perform test 3 again. Perform these steps:

1. First, log in to the database server using the following command:

    ```
    mysql -h 192.168.0.4 -u root -p
    ```

2. Then, issue the following commands from the MariaDB shell:

    ```
    USE employees;
    RESET QUERY CACHE;
    CREATE INDEX employees_emp_no ON employees(emp_no);
    CREATE INDEX salaries_emp_no ON salaries(emp_no);
    ```

3. After that, exit the MariaDB shell and run the test again to compare performance. The results are shown in the following screenshots and summarized against the previous example (without indexes) in the next table:

```
Benchmark
        Average number of seconds to run all queries: 0.043 seconds
        Minimum number of seconds to run all queries: 0.035 seconds
        Maximum number of seconds to run all queries: 0.055 seconds
        Number of clients running queries: 15
        Average number of queries per client: 10
```

Now, let's look at the results of the same test, but this time using indexes:

```
Benchmark
        Average number of seconds to run all queries: 0.038 seconds
        Minimum number of seconds to run all queries: 0.037 seconds
        Maximum number of seconds to run all queries: 0.046 seconds
        Number of clients running queries: 15
        Average number of queries per client: 10
```

TEST 3 (in seconds)	Node01 (without indexes)	Node01 (with indexes)
Average, all queries	0.043	0.038
Minimum, all queries	0.035	0.037
Maximum, all queries	0.055	0.046

Summarizing results of test 2 with and without indexes on node01

The preceding screenshots demonstrate that creating indexes on searchable fields will improve performance as it will prevent the server from having to go through all rows before returning the results.

Using query cache

In a MariaDB database server, the results of SELECT queries are stored in a query cache so that when the exact same operation is performed again, the results can be returned faster. This is precisely the case in most modern websites where similar queries are made over and over again (high-read and low-write environments).

So, how does this happen at the server level? If an incoming query is not found in the cache, it will be processed normally and then stored, along with its result set, in the query cache. Otherwise, the results are pulled from the cache, which makes it possible to complete the operation much faster than if it was processed normally.

In MariaDB, the query cache is enabled by default (SHOW VARIABLES LIKE 'query'query'_cache_type';), but its size is set to zero (SHOW VARIABLES LIKE 'query'query'_cache_size';), as indicated in the following screenshot:

```
MariaDB [(none)]> SHOW VARIABLES LIKE 'query_cache_type';
+------------------+-------+
| Variable_name    | Value |
+------------------+-------+
| query_cache_type | ON    |
+------------------+-------+
1 row in set (0.01 sec)

MariaDB [(none)]> SHOW VARIABLES LIKE 'query_cache_size';
+------------------+-------+
| Variable_name    | Value |
+------------------+-------+
| query_cache_size | 0     |
+------------------+-------+
1 row in set (0.00 sec)
```

For this reason, we need to set the query cache size variable to an appropriate value according to the use of our application. In the following screenshot, this variable is set to 100 KB (SET GLOBAL query_cache_size = 102400;), and we can see that the query cache size has been updated accordingly:

```
MariaDB [(none)]> SET GLOBAL query_cache_size = 102400;
Query OK, 0 rows affected (0.00 sec)

MariaDB [(none)]> SHOW VARIABLES LIKE 'query_cache_size';
+------------------+--------+
| Variable_name    | Value  |
+------------------+--------+
| query_cache_size | 102400 |
+------------------+--------+
1 row in set (0.00 sec)
```

Note that the right value for the query cache size will depend largely, if not entirely, on the needs of your specific case. Setting it too high will result in performance degradation as the system will have to allocate extra resources to manage a large cache. On the other hand, setting it to a very low value will cause at least some repeated queries to be processed normally and not be cached. In the preceding example, we allocated 100 KB of data as cache to store queries and their corresponding results.

For further details, refer to the MariaDB documentation (https://mariadb.com), specifically to the *Managing MariaDB/Optimization and tuning* section.

> The MariaDB documentation contains very helpful information to tune a database server starting from the ground up (all the way from the operating system level through query optimization). Other tools to increase performance and stability are MySQL tuner (http://mysqltuner.com/), MySQL Tuning Primer (https://launchpad.net/mysql-tuning-primer), and phpMyAdmin Advisor (https://www.phpmyadmin.net/). The last tool is available in the **Status** tab of a standard phpMyAdmin installation.

Moving to an A/A cluster

As you will recall from the introduction of *Chapter 3, A Closer Look at High Availability*, A/A clusters tend to provide higher availability as several nodes are actively running applications at the same time (which, by the way, requires that the necessary data for those applications be available simultaneously on all cluster members). The downside is that if one or more nodes go offline, the remaining ones are assigned extra processing load, thus negatively impacting the overall performance of the cluster.

That being said, let's examine briefly the required steps to convert our current A/P cluster to an A/A one. Make sure a STONITH resource has been defined (refer to chapter 3 for further details).

1. Enable STONITH resource by using the following command:

   ```
   pcs property set stonith-enabled=trueInstall
   ```

2. Install the additional software that will be needed for this:

   ```
   yum update && yum install gfs2-utils dlm
   ```

   As opposed to a traditional journaling filesystem such as `ext4` (which we have used for our filesystems up until this point in the book), you will need a way to ensure that all nodes are granted simultaneous access to the same block storage. **Global File System 2** (also known as **GFS2**) provides such a feature through its command-line tools, which are included in the `gfs2-utils` package.

3. In addition, the `dlm` package will install the **Distributed Lock Manager** (also known as **DLM**), a requirement in cluster filesystems to synchronize access to shared resources. Add (and clone) the Distributed Lock Manager as a cluster resource of the `ocf` class, pacemaker provider, and `controld` class:

   ```
   pcs cluster cib dlm_cfg
   ```

Measuring and Increasing Performance

```
pcs -f dlm_cfg resource create dlm ocf:pacemaker:controld op
monitor interval=60s
pcs -f dlm_cfg resource clone dlm clone-max=2 clone-node-max=1
```

4. Now, push the newly created resource to the CIB:

    `pcs cluster cib-push dlm_cfg`

5. Choose a replicated storage resource and create a `gfs2` filesystem on top of its associated device node.

    For example, let's use the `/dev/drbd0` device we created in *Chapter 4, Real-world Implementations of Clustering*. We will need to unmount it from the node with the DRBD primary role (most likely, `node01`) before we can create a `gfs2` filesystem on it:

    `umount /dev/drbd0`

    `mkfs.gfs2 -p lock_dlm -j 2 -t MyCluster:Web /dev/drbd0`

    Here, as you can see in the following screenshot, `MyCluster` is the original name of our cluster, `Web` is a random name, and the `-j` flag is used to indicate that the filesystem will use two journals (in this case one for each node - you will want to change this number if your cluster consists in more nodes). Finally, the `-p` option tells us that we are going to use the DLM provided by the kernel:

```
[root@node01 ~]# mkfs.gfs2 -p lock_dlm -j 2 -t MyCluster:Web /dev/drbd0
It appears to contain an existing filesystem (ext4)
This will destroy any data on /dev/drbd0
Are you sure you want to proceed? [y/n]y
Device:                    /dev/drbd0
Block size:                4096
Device size:               2.00 GB (523239 blocks)
Filesystem size:           2.00 GB (523236 blocks)
Journals:                  2
Resource groups:           9
Locking protocol:          "lock_dlm"
Lock table:                "MyCluster:Web"
UUID:                      1e8642b2-50bb-486d-0264-0ca928a48ab2
[root@node01 ~]#
```

    You will also need to change the `fstype` option of the `web_fs` resource from `ext4` (the original filesystem used when we first created it in *Chapter 4, Real-world Implementations of Clustering*) to `gfs2` in the PCS resource configuration:

    `pcs resource update web_fs fstype=gfs2`

Chapter 6

It is important to note that if the cluster attempts to start `web_fs` before `dlm-clone`, we will run into an issue (we cannot mount a `gfs2` filesystem if the `dlm` functionality is not present). Thus, we need to add colocation and ordering constraints so that `web_fs` will always start on the node where `dlm-clone` starts:

pcs constraint colocation add web_fs with dlm-clone INFINITY

and `dlm-clone` will be started before `web_fs`.

6. The `pcs constraint` order `dlm-clone` then `web_fsClone` the virtual IP address resource.

   Cloning the IP address will allow us to effectively use resources on both nodes, but at the same time, any given packet will be sent to only one node (thus, implementing a basic load-balancing method in our cluster):

   To do this, we will save the cluster configuration to a file named `load_balancing_cfg` and update such file with the :

   pcs cluster cib load_balancing_cfg

   You will notice from the pcs resource help that the clone operation allows you to specify certain options. In the following lines, `clone-max` specifies the number of nodes that host the `virtual_ip` resource (2 in this case), whereas clone-node-max indicates the number of resource instances each node is allowed to run. Next, `globally-unique` instructs the resource agent that each node is distinct from the rest and thus, handles distinct traffic as well. Finally, `clusterip_hash=sourceip` tells us that the packet's source IP address will be used to decide which node gets to process which request:

   pcs -f load_balancing_cfg resource clone virtual_ip clone-max=2 clone-node-max=2 globally-unique=true

   pcs -f load_balancing_cfg resource update virtual_ip clusterip_hash=sourceip

   The next steps consists of cloning the filesystem and Apache and/or MariaDB resources. Note that in order to allow two primaries in a DRBD device so that you can serve content from both at the same time, you will need to set the allow-two-primaries directive to yes (`allow-two-primaries yes;`) in the net section of the resource configuration file (`/etc/drbd.d/drbd0.res`, for example):

```
resource drbd0
  net {
    protocol C;
    allow-two-primaries yes;
  }
  ...
}
```

7. Once again, save the current CIB to a local file and add the clone resource information. In the next example, we will use `web_fs`, `web_drbd_clone` and `webserver`:

   ```
   pcs cluster cib current_cfg
   pcs -f current_cfg resource clone web_fs
   pcs -f current_cfg resource clone webserver
   ```

8. Now, `web_drbd` should be allowed to serve both instances as primary or master:

   ```
   pcs -f current_cfg resource update web_drbd_clone master-max=2
   ```

9. Then, activate the new configuration:

   ```
   pcs cluster cib-push current_cfg
   ```

10. Last but not least, you need to keep in mind that you will need to set the value of the resource stickiness to 0 in order for it to return an instance to its original node after a failover. To do so, refer to the *Performing a failover* section this same chapter.

You can now proceed to force a failover as usual, and test the resource availability. Unfortunately, this is not possible in a Virtualbox environment as I have explained previously. However, it's entirely possible if you are able to build your cluster with real hardware and an actual STONITH device.

Summary

In this last chapter, we set up a couple of performance testing tools for the example services that you need to make highly available in your cluster, and provided a few suggestions to optimize their performance separately as well. Note that those suggestions are not intended to represent an exhaustive list of tuning methods, but a starting point instead. We have also provided the overall instructions so that you can convert an A/P cluster into an A/A one.

Finally, keep in mind that this book was written using virtual machines instead of specialized hardware. Thus, we have run into some associated limitations, such as the lack for real STONITH devices that would otherwise have allowed us to actually demonstrate the functionalities of an A/A cluster. However, the principles outlined in this book will undoubtedly be a guide to set up your own clusters, whether you are experimenting with virtual machines as well or using real hardware.

Best of success in your endeavors!

Index

Symbols

7789 TCP port 62

A

A/A (Active/Active) cluster 38
A/P (Active/Passive) cluster
    about 38
    converting to 119-122
Apache
    DRBD resource, testing 79, 80
    DRBD resource, using 76-79
Apache MPM Common directives
    URL 115

C

CentOS
    downloading 3
    URL 3
CentOS 7
    about 2
    installing 5-7
    nodes, setting up 4, 5
    URL 2
    using 2
cluster
    configuring, with PCS GUI 51, 52
    virtual IP, setting up 33
Cluster Information Base (CIB) 66
clustering
    about 1, 2
    CentOS 7, using 2
    Linux, using 2
    required packages, installing 10

clustering services
    configuring 18
    enabling 18-20
    starting 18
    troubleshooting 20
cluster resource
    about 33
    problems, troubleshooting 85
    virtual IP, adding 33
    web servers, configuring 72-76
cluster tests
    failover, performing 111-113
    fields, retrieving from records 109, 110
    JOIN operations, performing 110
    performing 108, 109
Corosync 11, 18

D

database resource
    indexes, creating 116, 117
    performance optimization 116
    query cache, using 117, 118
database servers
    installing 70-72
datagrams 21
Dell Remote Access Controller (DRAC) 48
Designated Controller (DC) 32, 49
Distributed Lock Manager (DLM) 119
Distributed Replicated Block Device
        (DRBD)
    about 56
    adding, as PCS cluster resource 66-70
    availability 58-60
    configuring 60-65
    installing 56

DRBD resource
  mounting 76-79
  testing, with Apache 79, 80
  used, with Apache 76-79
Dynamic Shared Objects (DSOs) 113

E

ELRepo repository 58-60
Employees database
  downloading 104-108
  installing 104-108
  setting up 103
  URL 104

F

failover 38-43
fencing
  about 44
  malfunctioning nodes, isolating 43-45

G

Global File System 2 (GFS2) 119

H

high-availability database
  setting up, with replicated storage 80-84
high availability (HA) 2
high-performance cluster (HPC) 2

I

iLO (Integrated Lights Out) 48
indexes
  creating 116, 117
Internet Group Management Protocol (IGMP) 21
Internet model 17

K

key-based authentication
  setting up, for SSH access 14, 15

L

LAMP stack 70
Linbit
  URL 62
Linux
  using 2
Logical Volume (LV) 81
Logical Volume Manager (LVM) 58

M

man journalctl
  URL 20
MariaDB
  URL 119
members 1
modprobe command 58
mysqlslap tool
  --concurrency flag 109
  --create-schema flag 109
  --delimiter flag 109
  --iterations flag 109
  --number-of-queries flag 109
  --query flag 109
  about 109
MySQL tuner
  URL 119
MySQL Tuning Primer
  URL 119

N

Nagios 89
network security
  fundamentals 20
  traffic, allowing between nodes 21-25
nodes
  about 1
  status, monitoring 89-92
nodes, CentOS 7
  CentOS 7, installing 5-7
  network infrastructure, setting up 7-10
  setting up 4, 5

P

Pacemaker 11, 18
packages
  installing, for clustering 10
  key-based authentication, setting up for SSH access 14, 15
  software components, using 11-14
PCS
  about 11, 18
  authentication, managing 28-33
  cluster, creating 28-33
  setting up 25-28
PCS cluster resource
  Distributed Replicated Block Device (DRBD), adding 66-70
PCS GUI
  cluster, configuring 51, 52
performance optimization, cluster
  about 113
  Apache children, limiting 115
  Apache processes, limiting 115
  Apache's configuration 113, 114
  Apache's settings 113, 114
  database resource 116
  modules, disabling 115
  modules, loading 115
phpMyAdmin Advisor
  URL 119
Physical Volume (PV) 81
protocols 17
ps command 89

Q

query cache
  using 117, 118
quorum 49-51

R

replicated storage
  high-availability database, setting up 80-84
resource agent 113
resources
  availability of core components, checking 100, 101

  monitoring 92-98
  starting issues, monitoring 98, 99

S

SELinux (Security Enhanced Linux) 25
server status page
  URL 73
Shoot The Other Node In The Head (STONITH) 4, 34
  device, configuring 45-49
  device, installing 45-49
simply gateway [192.168.0.1] 7
Single Point Of Failure (SPOF) 49
software components
  Corosync 11
  Pacemaker 11
  PCS 11
  using 11-14
split-brain 49
SSH access
  key-based authentication, setting up 14, 15
standard Centos package manager yum 3
storage
  setting up 55-58

T

top command 89
Transmission Control Protocol (TCP) 21

U

Usage DRBD.org
  URL 61
User Datagram Protocol (UDP) 21

V

VirtualBox
  installing 4
  URL 4
  virtual hard disk, adding 59

[125]

virtual IP
 adding, as cluster resource 33
 setting up, for cluster 33
 status, viewing 34
Volume Group (VG) 81

W

web servers
 configuring, as cluster resource 72-76
 installing 70-72

Z

Zabbix 89

Thank you for buying
CenOS High Performance

About Packt Publishing

Packt, pronounced 'packed', published its first book, *Mastering phpMyAdmin for Effective MySQL Management*, in April 2004, and subsequently continued to specialize in publishing highly focused books on specific technologies and solutions.

Our books and publications share the experiences of your fellow IT professionals in adapting and customizing today's systems, applications, and frameworks. Our solution-based books give you the knowledge and power to customize the software and technologies you're using to get the job done. Packt books are more specific and less general than the IT books you have seen in the past. Our unique business model allows us to bring you more focused information, giving you more of what you need to know, and less of what you don't.

Packt is a modern yet unique publishing company that focuses on producing quality, cutting-edge books for communities of developers, administrators, and newbies alike. For more information, please visit our website at www.packtpub.com.

About Packt Open Source

In 2010, Packt launched two new brands, Packt Open Source and Packt Enterprise, in order to continue its focus on specialization. This book is part of the Packt Open Source brand, home to books published on software built around open source licenses, and offering information to anybody from advanced developers to budding web designers. The Open Source brand also runs Packt's Open Source Royalty Scheme, by which Packt gives a royalty to each open source project about whose software a book is sold.

Writing for Packt

We welcome all inquiries from people who are interested in authoring. Book proposals should be sent to author@packtpub.com. If your book idea is still at an early stage and you would like to discuss it first before writing a formal book proposal, then please contact us; one of our commissioning editors will get in touch with you.

We're not just looking for published authors; if you have strong technical skills but no writing experience, our experienced editors can help you develop a writing career, or simply get some additional reward for your expertise.

CentOS 6 Linux Server Cookbook

ISBN: 978-1-84951-902-1   Paperback: 374 pages

A practical guide to installing, configuring, and administering the CentOS community-based enterprise server

1. Delivering comprehensive insight into CentOS server with a series of starting points that show you how to build, configure, maintain and deploy the latest edition of one of the world's most popular community based enterprise servers.

2. Providing beginners and more experienced individuals alike with the opportunity to enhance their knowledge by delivering instant access to a library of recipes that addresses all aspects of CentOS server and put you in control.

CentOS System Administration Essentials

ISBN: 978-1-78398-592-0   Paperback: 174 pages

Become an efficient CentOS administrator by acquiring real-world knowledge of system setup and configuration

1. Centralize user accounts in openLDAP and understand how Directory can be at the back-end of many services.

2. Learning Puppet to centralize server configuration will free up your time as configuration is handled just once on the configuration server.

3. A step-by-step guide that covers the very popular Linux Distribution CentOS 6.5 with easy-to-follow instructions.

Please check **www.PacktPub.com** for information on our titles

CentOS High Availability

ISBN: 978-1-78528-248-5   Paperback: 174 pages

Leverage the power of high availability clusters on CentOS Linux, the enterprise-class, open source operating system

1. Install, configure, and manage a multi-node cluster running on CentOS Linux.

2. Manage your cluster resources and learn how to start, stop, and migrate resources from one host to another.

3. Designed as a step-by-step guide, this book will help you become a master of cluster nodes, cluster resources, and cluster services on CentOS 6 and CentOS 7.

Troubleshooting CentOS

ISBN: 978-1-78528-982-8   Paperback: 190 pages

A practical guide to troubleshooting the CentOS 7 community-based enterprise server

1. Gain exposure to insider tips and techniques to quickly detect the reason for poor network/storage performance.

2. Troubleshooting methodologies, defining, and isolating problems.

3. Identify key issues that impact performance, storage, scalability, capacity.

Please check **www.PacktPub.com** for information on our titles

Made in the USA
Middletown, DE
18 October 2016